A Guide for Educational Policy Governance

Other Books by M. Scott Norton

The Principal as a Learning-Leader: Motivating Students by Emphasizing Achievement
Competency-Based Leadership: A Guide for High Performance in the Role of the School Principal
Teachers with the Magic: Great Teachers Change Students' Lives
The Changing Landscape of School Leadership: Recalibrating the School Principalship
The Legal World of the School Principal: What Leaders Need to Know about School Law
Guiding Curriculum Development: The Need to Return to Local Control
Guiding the Human Resources Function in Education: New Issues, New Needs

A Guide for Educational Policy Governance

Effective Leadership for Policy Development

M. Scott Norton

ROWMAN & LITTLEFIELD
Lanham • Boulder • New York • London

Published by Rowman & Littlefield
A wholly owned subsidiary of The Rowman & Littlefield Publishing Group, Inc.
4501 Forbes Boulevard, Suite 200, Lanham, Maryland 20706
www.rowman.com

Unit A, Whitacre Mews, 26-34 Stannary Street, London SE11 4AB

Copyright © 2017 by M. Scott Norton

All rights reserved. No part of this book may be reproduced in any form or by any electronic or mechanical means, including information storage and retrieval systems, without written permission from the publisher, except by a reviewer who may quote passages in a review.

British Library Cataloguing in Publication Information Available

Library of Congress Cataloging-in-Publication Data Is Available

ISBN 978-1-4758-3559-5 (cloth: alk. paper)
ISBN 978-1-4758-3560-1 (pbk: alk. paper)
ISBN 978-1-4758-3561-8 (electronic)

∞™ The paper used in this publication meets the minimum requirements of American National Standard for Information Sciences—Permanence of Paper for Printed Library Materials, ANSI/NISO Z39.48-1992.

Printed in the United States of America

Contents

Preface		vii
1	A Pathway to Effective Policy and Administrative Regulation Development	1
2	Effective Use: Putting the School Policies and Regulations to Work	29
3	Policy and Regulation Development: The Difference That It Makes	55
4	Impact of Federal Laws, State Statutes, and the Courts on Local School Policy	83
Glossary		113
About the Author		119

Preface

WHY THE BOOK WAS WRITTEN

The development of school district policies and regulations is the most important responsibility of school boards nationally. In addition, the work of a school district's administration looms important for the effective implementation of school policy. Effective school operations depend on a viable system of policy development. Effective policy development is the crux of successful school operations. At the outset, we applaud the great work that many school boards are doing to implement effective governance policy systems in their school districts.

However, many school districts nationally purchase their policies from their state's school board association. This boilerplate procedure prohibits the ability of staff personnel to become committed to the directives set forth in policies for which they had no input. Control of school operations depends greatly on the body that controls policy adoption. When federal mandates, state statutes, court rulings, and state school board associations are primarily responsible for establishing a local school district's policy system, internal apathy on the part of staff personnel is fostered, and local governance control is inhibited.

In addition, empirical evidence makes it clear that many local boards and administrative personnel lack the knowledge and skill for developing an effective policy system in their school districts. This fact is revealed by such data that show the number of school districts that have yet to establish an effective policy system. Members of school faculties tend to misuse terminology in regard to policies, regulations, and bylaws. It is common, for example, to hear a school principal speak of his or her school policies or to hear a school board member speak of the school district's rules. Few professional personnel know the methods for codifying school policies and regulations.

This book sets forth information and guidelines for remedying the foregoing problems. Each employee needs to be knowledgeable of the importance of policies and regulations for effective school operations and be able to converse accurately with policy and regulation language and strategies. Such knowledge not only is of concern to school superintendents and other administrative leaders, but it is the concern of professional and classified employees of the school system as well. Effective policy governance requires ongoing policy awareness strategies whereby all school personnel are responsible for reading and understanding the policies and regulations pertaining to their behavior and work responsibilities. The foregoing status sets forth the primary reasons why this book was written.

THE ORGANIZATION OF THE BOOK

The content of the book is presented in four relevant chapters. Each chapter includes a primary goal, a reader-friendly style, reader quizzes, snapshots, discussion questions, case studies, references, and section exercises to engage the reader and foster extended learning activities. Extensive consideration is given to the organization of a policy system, codification strategies, local control leadership, and the influence of federal laws, state statutes, court rulings, and governance policy models on policy development at the local school level.

Chapter 1 of the book is designed to establish the groundwork for policy development. A brief historical background of policy development is presented, and the policy systems of the National School Boards Association and the Davies-Brickell policy system are discussed in detail. In addition, the benefits of an effective policy system are discussed. In chapter 2, the implementation of policy codifications systems is presented in depth. The use of policy manuals and policy awareness strategies is emphasized. Chapter 3 presents models of exemplary policy systems and best practices of school board planning and designing of policy systems in the school district. Chapter 4 discusses the influence of the federal government, state legislatures, and the courts on the school district's policy control. The pros and cons of policy controls on educational programs by these agencies are discussed. Both traditional and governance policy models are described in depth.

A special feature of the book is the use of exercises, quizzes, and discussion questions to increase the reader's engagement in the book's content and to foster the reader's interest in extended learning. Relevant court studies, case studies, and each chapter's key ideas and recommendations are included in an effort to meet this objective.

Chapter 1

A Pathway to Effective Policy and Administrative Regulation Development

Primary Chapter Goal: To define and illustrate the basic terms of educational governance, including district policy, administrative regulation, school board bylaws, state and federal laws, and to underscore the importance of governance policies in promoting educational goals and objectives.

What is a school district policy and an administrative regulation? We asked this question of a large number of practicing educators, and none was able to give satisfactory definitions or describe the related characteristics of these two terms. The term "policy" is commonly misused by practicing administrators; school principals, for example, often refer to their local school policies when referring to a local school rule or a school district administrative regulation. These facts should not be surprising. School district policies and administrative regulations commonly are boilerplate products developed by external agencies such as state or national school boards associations.

Thus, many school districts in the same state have the same policies, and therein lies the reason that most policy manuals sit on the shelves gathering dust in teachers' classrooms or wasting away on some Web page. Teachers commonly have little or no input in their school district's policies and regulations and therefore have little interest, knowledge, or commitment relative to these *governance* documents. Chapter 1 centers on changing this perspective by underscoring the paramount importance of these governance documents and supporting a major increase in policy leadership at the local school level. Local school district involvement in specific policy development all too often is limited.

An Explanation of Model Policies

Policy development is an ongoing, time-consuming, and difficult task. Thus, many school districts nationally would struggle to keep a policy system relevant and up to date. Nationally, the local school boards' answer to this problem has been to purchase their policies from the state's school board association. The local school board association writes the school policies for each participating school district but points out that through the adoption process a school board can change or replace existing policies and also notes that the state association's policies are to be adopted only after review and revision to suit each school district. Unfortunately, such revision is perfunctory at best.

A school district in Arkansas can subscribe to the state's school boards association policy service, which is $1,100 per year for three years, and renewal is $950 per year for three years. The state school boards association monitors changes in state and federal laws and the Arkansas Department of Education's rules for necessary changes or new policy development (Arkansas School Boards Association, 2015).

As of 1970, at least half of the nation's twenty thousand school boards had not established a written policy statement or kept one updated with new methods (Dickinson, 1970). Unfortunately, a recent communication with the National School Boards Association (NSBA) indicated that an update of the status of policy systems in the nation's school districts had not been undertaken.

Chapter 1 centers on defining significant governance terms appropriately and discussing their historical significance and strategic importance in school districts and local school operations. At the outset, we want to engage you in the subject at hand by asking you to participate in two activities. First, however, it is necessary to note the fact that policy definitions do tend to differ somewhat from state to state.

For example, the aforementioned early leaders of policy classification identified the term "administrative *regulations*" similarly. Later, the state of Arkansas used the term "procedures" rather than "regulations" in its policy statement. That is, the state of Arkansas viewed regulations as procedures stemming from state or federal statutes rather than administrative regulations for carrying out a school board policy. Arkansas's definition for procedures is exactly the definition most commonly used for identifying administrative regulations. In addition, published books and articles not only define policy terms differently, but also present policy governance procedures much differently.

Most authorities view school board policies as the purposes, ends, or aims of the school district's educational program. However, an early publication by Rich (1974) set forth procedures for implementing public school governance policy. We cite the following reference to illustrate one reason for the confusion that exists in policy development nationally.

According to Rich (1974), "The function of policy, however, differs from that of aims. Policy essentially serves to regulate institutions and organizations; it provides orderly procedures for day-by-day operations and thereby affords a sense of continuity. . . . The rules and regulations that govern the operations of organizations can be considered to be forms of policy" (p. 16). Such statements confuse and mislead the efforts to foster a clear understanding of policy and administrative regulation development in education. Rich's view of governance policy is completely opposite that of the more recent descriptions set forth by Carver's governance model that is discussed in-depth in chapter 4.

Chapter 1 Pre-Quiz

In the following pre-quiz, we ask the questions: What is a school board policy? What is an administrative regulation? What is a bylaw? Use the space following each of the following entries to write your brief response to each statement or do so on a separate sheet of paper. This is a self-evaluation "check," and only you will know the result.

MY DEFINITON OF A POLICY IS AS FOLLOWS:

MY DEFINITION OF AN ADMINISTRATIVE REGULATION IS AS FOLLOWS:

MY DEFINITION OF A BYLAW IS AS FOLLOWS:

Now, check your responses with the following definitions of policy, regulation, and bylaw.

A POLICY—is a general statement as to *what* is to be accomplished. It is a directive and leaves room for administrative discretion. It is a principle that relates closely to purposes, goals, or aims to be achieved.

AN ADMINISTRATIVE REGULATION OR PROCEDURE—is a specific statement indicating *how* a policy is to be implemented. It is specific and tends to limit personal discretion by calling for exact interpretation and execution.

A BYLAW—is a rule governing the school board's internal operations. It is one that a board of education uses to direct its own work.

Criteria for Determining Policies, Regulations, and Bylaws

Briefly review the foregoing term definitions and then proceed to set forth at least two criteria that identify a policy, an administrative regulation, and a bylaw.

List at least two specific criteria for identifying a policy:

1.
2.
3.

List at least two specific criteria for identifying an administrative regulation:

1.
2.
3.

List at least two specific criteria for identifying a bylaw:

1.
2.
3.

Criteria for Identifying a Policy, Regulation, Bylaw and Rule

A Policy is:

1. an assertion of a goal(s), purpose(s), or an aim(s);
2. related to a general area of prime importance;
3. equivalent to legislation;
4. applicable over long periods of time;
5. a broad statement that allows for freedom of interpretation and execution;
6. mainly the concern of the school board;
7. a strategy undertaken to solve or ameliorate a problem or need;
8. concerned with topics of vital interest to the citizenry;
9. related to the question of *what* to do.

A Regulation is:

1. related to a specific problem or area of administration; it is a procedure to carry out a policy;
2. mainly the concern of the professional staff;
3. a precise statement calling for exact interpretation and execution;
4. related to the question of *how* to do;
5. executive in nature but ultimately under the legislative authority of the school board.

A Bylaw is:

1. a combination of laws and parliamentary procedures;
2. like any other rule, which specifies required actions that leave little room for individual judgments;
3. a rule that relates to internal operations of the board of education;
4. related to the question of how the school board will govern itself.

A Rule is:

1. a standard statement, other than a policy or regulation, that is set forth by an administrative unit within the school district or a local school for the primary purpose of implementing an administrative regulation;
2. a statement of behavior and/or activity that specifies personnel or student actions but does not conflict with either school policies or administrative regulations;
3. related to the question of how a regulation such as student control is to be enforced in a school environment.

A FEW CLARIFICATIONS REGARDING POLICIES AND REGULATIONS

We have noted that policies are principles/aims adopted by the school board to underscore a purpose the school district wants to achieve. Policies are general in nature and call for a course of action to be taken by the school administration in meeting the desired purposes of the educational program. In some cases, a policy might provide sufficient direction so that a follow-up regulation is not needed. The reverse of this possibility is not true. That is, an administrative regulation is not to appear unto itself; it always is written to indicate how an adopted policy is to be implemented.

In practice, policies and regulations are sometimes confused. When this occurs, school boards are placed in a position of approving regulations that are interwoven within statements of policy. In some instances, school boards approve policies with regulatory components for lack of understanding. On the other hand, a board might approve detailed regulations because the matter is especially sensitive and such action is in the best interests of the school community.

In any case, sometimes it is just difficult to separate policy from regulation. Differences between the two terms are sometimes "blurred," and follow-up clarification is needed to expedite the application of the policy statement in practice. Nevertheless, when the circumstances of law require board approval, a statement with regulatory implications is approved as policy. In addition, whenever the board has included a regulation within an intended policy, it is considered as a policy. Specifically, in section 8000 or section B of a school district's policy manual on board operating procedures, many of the subsections and divisions commonly are revealed as regulations rather than meeting the strict definition of policies.

A CHECK ON WHAT YOU KNOW NOW

After quickly reviewing the criteria related to a policy, regulation, and bylaw, circle the correct response for each of the following ten entries as being a policy (p), regulation (r), or bylaw (b). Do not be concerned with the "advisability" of the entry because the entries are used for illustrative purposes only and not as good policies, regulations, or bylaws appropriate for educational purposes.

1. No school board standing committees shall be appointed to perform any of the school board actions (p, r, b).
2. Teachers will remain on campus for a minimum of thirty minutes after their last class of the day except to attend special school meetings, supervise assigned club sponsorships, or other special meetings or requirements of the school and/or school district (p, r, b).
3. The student/teacher ratio for elementary school classes will be 24:1 (p, r, b).
4. Special needs children will receive appropriate instruction (p, r, b).
5. Don't shoot until you have a sure shot (p, r, b).
6. Don't shoot until you see the whites of their eyes (p, r, b).
7. All capital property valued at $100 or more will be inventoried annually (p, r, b).
8. School athletes will meet school academic standards (p, r, b).
9. Transportation to and from school will be provided to all students who are determined to need it (p, r, b).
10. School principals are responsible for establishing procedures for student control (p, r, b).

The Answers for the Pre-Quiz

1. Entry #1 is a bylaw (b). It centers on the way the school board will govern itself.
2. Entry #2 is an administrative regulation (r). It is specific in setting forth a procedure for on-site attendance and leaves little or no room for discretion.
3. Entry #3 is an administrative school regulation (r). The statement is quite specific and leaves no room for interpretation. It sets forth a requirement to be followed for class size.
4. Entry #4 is a policy (p). It establishes an aim for serving special needs students but leaves much room for school leaders to determine what constitutes the best educational program for its students with special needs.
5. Entry #5 would constitute a policy (p). Primarily, it gives the shooter discretion in determining when a good shot is ready. The shooter is to determine when he or she has a sure shot.

6. Entry #6 is an administrative regulation (r). Primarily, it gives specific directions for when the shot is to be made: "when you see the whites of their eyes." It gives the shooter specific directions on how to determine when to shoot.
7. Entry #7 is an administrative regulation (r). Each piece of school property valued at $100 or more must be inventoried; no discretion is implied in the statement. The statement answers the question of how to determine what is to be inventoried. A policy statement would give the school personnel discretion in determining the value of capital property on hand and if it should be inventoried.
8. Entry #8 is a policy (p) because it leaves considerable discretion for local school personnel to determine the required standards that must be met. The wisdom of such a policy is not the point. Rather, the statement meets the question of what to do regarding standards for school athletes based on differences in school culture and program activities.
9. Entry #9 is a policy (p). The statement is clear as to its aim but leaves room for determining appropriate procedures for its implementation to the local schools.
10. Entry #10 is a policy (p). The question of what to do is clearly established, and the matter of how to carry out the policy, *discretion*, is left to the local administrators.

HOW SCHOOL BOARDS GOVERN THEMSELVES

The Dwight Public Schools #230 & 232 (undated) have shown outstanding attention to school policy development. For this reason, we will extend the importance of bylaws for purposeful board governance in the following section of the Dwight school bylaws. Below illustrates one entry of the school board's bylaws relative to board governance.

Figure 1.1: Bylaw for School Board Governance—Dwight Public Schools School Board

School Board Governance

The District is governed by a School Board consisting of 7 members. The Board's powers and duties include the authority to adopt, enforce, and monitor all policies for the management and governance of the District's schools.

Official action by the Board may only occur at a duly called and legally conducted meeting at which a quorum is physically present.

As stated in the Board member oath of office prescribed by the School Code, a Board member has no legal authority as an individual.

LEGAL REFERENCE: 5ILCS 120/1.02 105 ILCS 5/10-1, 5/10-=10, 5/10-12, 5/10-16.5, 5/10-16.7 and 5/10-20.5

CROSS REFERENC E: 1:10 (School District Legal Status) 2:20 (Powers and Duties of the School Board; Indemnification), (Board Member Oath and

Conduct), 2:120 (Board Member Development), 2:200 (Types of School Board Meetings), 2:220 (School Board Meeting Procedures)
ADOPTED: August 6, 2014

Source: Dwight Public Schools #230 & 232, Dwight, Illinois.

The bylaw above underscores several characteristics of effective bylaws. For example, it is specific in focusing on how the school board will govern itself; it underscores a parliamentary procedure relative to the school board's official actions; it leaves little or no room for implementation or personal judgment; and it is related to internal operations of the school board.

What Factors and Obstacles Keep School Boards from Developing a Viable Policy System?

Reported Obstacles to Getting Policies in Writing

1. Time factors, including the difficulty of the task at hand.
2. Lack of administrative leadership, including lack of know-how.
3. School board opinions/attitudes such as viewing policies and regulations as being restrictive: an attitude that policies tend to tie the hands of the board by "freezing a course of action in place."
4. Frequent school board member turnover inhibits continuity of board operations.
5. High cost of consultant and legal services.
6. "Mandated" policy development services tend to control board initiative.
7. Increasing mandates from state and federal agencies that require specific school board actions that lead to loss of local control.
8. Lack of knowledge regarding school board policies and administrative regulations, their definitions, purposes, and benefits.
9. A belief that "we just do not need policies."

THE BENEFITS OF POLICY DEVELOPMENT FAR OUTWEIGH THE TIME AND EFFORT TO DEVELOP THEM

What are the benefits of a viable set of school policies and regulations? Who benefits? Once again, we ask you to take a few minutes to list what you believe are the real benefits of policies and regulations. Be as specific as possible in your response. Following your listing, we will list several significant benefits of policies and regulations for comparison purposes. List your thoughts about how policies and regulations benefit your school district and then compare your entries with those that follow your listing.

1.
2.
3.
4.
5.
6.

HOW A POLICY SYSTEM WORKS FOR US

We submit that school policies and administrative regulations benefit the school board, school district, the local schools, the school superintendent, the professional and classified staff, and the school district stakeholders in the following ways. "Written and continuously updated policies are the sine qua non of a soundly organized and efficiently operated school" (Dickinson, 1970, p. 1). We emphasize throughout the book that policy development is a process and not a product. The practice of reviewing the school district's policies once a year is an administrative misconception.

Viable policies and regulations:

1. establish the division of labor between the school board and the professional and classified staffs. When responsibilities are well defined and understood, each level of school operations is more able to accomplish its work effectively, accountability is facilitated, and purposes are more likely to be achieved.
2. establish the basis for intelligent decision making and direct decision making at proper levels within the school system.
3. inform all concerned as to the goals and objectives of the school system and provide discretion for the administration to determine how these objectives are to be met.
4. are a foundation for effective system communication both internally and externally.
5. avoid costly trial and error. Policy answers the question of what is to be done, and regulations answer the question of how the aim is to be accomplished.
6. serve an important legal function for the school board, school district administrators, and the professional and classified staff personnel. Policies ensure legal compliance, establish school district aims, delegate administrative authority, and define operating conditions/limits.

7. focus on settling purposes/questions that often are encountered in daily operations.
8. foster improved school-community relations due to an assurance of responsible school board action.
9. promote and facilitate school board operations and effective transition when changes in school board membership take place.
10. support the processes of evaluation and accountability on the part of the school board and professional staff.
11. save time, money, and effort by providing answers to what is to be done/accomplished.
12. promote and facilitate the assessment of school board and school district practices.

Thus, everyone benefits from a viable set of policies and regulations. Policy gives the school board the control it needs to direct the school program. Administrative regulations give the school superintendent and staff personnel more freedom to accomplish their responsibilities by allowing the discretionary behavior needed to innovate, facilitate, and evaluate their position responsibilities.

GOVERNANCE CHECKS AND BALANCES

School boards are given their authority by the state legislature. Thus, the school board serves as a legislative, not executive, body. The administrative and professional staff represents the executive body and is given its authority by the school board, state legislature, and the courts. That is, the judicial branch of the school district is based on the existing legal bodies of government such as the state statutes and the courts that are revealed in the policies and regulations approved by the school board and developed cooperatively in the school district's administrative regulations.

HOW POLICIES AND REGULATIONS ARE DEVELOPED

The model shown in figure 1.2 illustrates the development of goals, policies, and regulations. Educational goals are statements that set forth the purposes of the school system. Educational goals are developed through cultural sanctions, professional judgments, and lay judgments. Cultural sanctions are the set of important assumptions, beliefs, values, and attitudes that members of the school community share. Professional judgments are the views and knowledge of effective educators and others who are members of the school community. Lay judgment is found within the school community by its members in terms of their views of education's goals and objectives.

School district policies are developed through school board action that is guided by state legislative statutes and the leadership of school administrative personnel. Policies are local adaptations of stated educational goals. Only the school board can adopt school policy. However, federal and state mandates and statutes commonly are inserted into local school district policy verbatim. Court decisions tend to influence/control a school district's policies as well. Administrative regulations and rules are developed through professional judgments and administrative decisions regarding how a board policy can best be implemented.

The school superintendent's leadership is witnessed in his or her ability to provide up-to-date information to the school board relative to issues and needs to consider new policies or revisions, but not to draft the policies for the school board's consideration and approval. Drafting policies is the responsibility of the school board; the school superintendent and professional staff serve to draft the administrative regulations for implementing the policies and submitting them to the school board for approval.

Thus, administrative regulations commonly are viewed as being mainly the concern of the professional staff. Nevertheless, the development of administrative regulations by the professional staff is done only through the delegation of this authority by the school board. This is one reason why it is always wise for the school superintendent and professional staff personnel to have the school board examine and assess all administrative regulations to be implemented.

Such action serves two primary purposes. First, it provides an opportunity to determine if the school administrative leaders are working to implement the policies set forth by the school board. Second, it serves to show the school board that the administration is doing its job.

We note that some policy models contend that it is a natural phenomenon to discuss regulations whenever policy is discussed; that is, they are inextricably related.

The following quotation is from an article by Meador (2016, January 17) on the topic of writing policies and procedures. We submit that the recommended procedures are opposite of best practices.

"Writing policies and procedures for schools is a part of an administrator's job. . . . The first thing that has to happen is that a rough draft of the policy has to be written by a Principal or other school administrator" (p. 1). Such statements have the school administrators doing the work of the school board. The writing of procedures for school board approval is another matter. Administrative regulations are within the jurisdiction of the professional staff.

Figure 1.2: Conceptual Model of the Development of Goals, Policies, and Administrative Regulations

Cultural Sanctions
Professional Judgments
Lay Judgments
V
V
V
Educational Goals Are Developed
School Board Action with Administrative Leadership
Local Adaptation to Goals
V
V
V
School Board Policies Are Developed
Administrative Decisions
Professional Judgments
V
V
V
Administrative Regulations Are Developed and Implemented

HOW POLICIES AND ADMINISTRATIVE REGULATIONS ARE ORGANIZED (CODIFIED)

Most every educator is familiar with the Dewey Decimal System, a proprietary library classification system first published in the United States by Melvil Dewey in 1876. It has been revised and expanded through twenty-three major editions, the latest in 2011, and has grown from a four-page pamphlet in 1876 with fewer than one thousand classes to a four-volume set (Wikipedia, 2016, October). One can imagine the problems of dealing with literally millions of books in a library without some way to organize them.

Similarly, it became clear that the increasing volumes of school board policies and administrative regulations needed organization in order to make them readily available for easy reference. Recognizing the importance of written policies to efficient public school operations, the NSBA between 1958 and 1960 produced, in cooperation with the National Education Association, the *Reference Manual on Written School Board Policies* and a companion publication, *How to Develop Written Policies: A Guide to Procedures* (Dickinson, 1970).

During the same period, the Davies-Brickell *System of School Board Policymaking and Administration* (1958) was developed in the school district of

Manhasset, New York, under a grant from the Kellogg Foundation, and was published by Croft Educational Services of New London, Connecticut. The Davies-Brickell system is considered by authorities America's first commercially produced school board policy-making system. Since its appearance in 1958, school districts have implemented this system extensively or used the system with a few changes that served the district's operational programs.

Without question, the initiative of local school districts to develop policy manuals was a slow process. Even today, far too many school districts in the United States fail to have up-to-date, written policy manuals. Even where school districts do have policy manuals, the large majority are boilerplate products developed by associations outside the local school community.

The Davies-Brickell codification system for policies and regulations, or Arabic system, and the NEPN (National Education Policy Network)/NSBA, or Alpha system, led the way in the development of classification systems for school board policies and regulations. In this chapter, we focus on these two policy/codification systems but will refer to several ways in which these basic classification systems have been changed, extended, and altered by school districts throughout the nation. Virtually every school board codification system is based on one of the two foregoing policy classification systems.

Foundational Developments: A Brief History of Policy/Regulation Classification

In a comprehensive report on the development of a school board policy development system by William Dickinson in 1970, the following facts were reported:

1. Using data collected in 1959, approximately two-thirds of the school boards sampled reported that they had a policy manual.
2. In the spring of 1968, the National School Boards Association surveyed fifty state departments of education. Only seven of twenty-four state departments responding to a question indicated that a majority of local boards maintained a well-developed system for keeping written policies up to date.
3. The need for assistance by departments in 1968 was further demonstrated by the fact that only 25 percent of local school boards reported having a well-developed policy-making system.
4. Ninety-two percent of the school boards reporting expressed interest in getting ongoing and more comprehensive assistance from the NSBA regarding policy school policy/codification procedures.
5. By the end of the 1960s, an NSBA survey revealed that, although some progress in policy development had been achieved, as many as one-half of the nation's twenty thousand school boards either maintained no manual of written policies or they were employing inadequate methods for recording policy decisions.

6. In 2016, an inquiry was directed to the NSBA regarding the percentage of school districts nationally that had an effective system of policy development. The association was not able to answer the question.

POLICY CODIFICATION: HOW CLASSIFICATION SYSTEMS WORK

The Arabic Davies-Brickell system is based on nine major logical series with each one assigned a section number. Note that numbers are used in this classification system (table 1.1).

Keep in mind that these nine major sections were first set forth in 1958 by Davies and Brickell. In 1970, the National School Boards Association adopted the Alpha classification series as follows (table 1.2).

Since 1970, NSBA has revised its classification descriptors, and the various states have either adopted the NSBA model or changed the descriptors to

Table 1.1 Davies-Brickell System

Policy Section	Section Number
Community Relations	1000
Administration	2000
Business and Noninstructional Operations	3000
Personnel	4000
Students	5000
Instruction	6000
New Construction	7000
Internal Board Policies	8000
Bylaws	9000

Table 1.2 National School Boards Association System

Policy Letter	Policy Section
A	Foundations and Basic Commitments
B	School Board Operations
C	General School Administration
D	Fiscal Management
E	Business Management/Support Services
F	Facility Development
G	Personnel
H	Negotiations/Meet and Confer
I	Instructional Program
J	Students
K	School Community Relations
L	Educational Agencies Relations
M	Relations with Other Organizational Agencies

A Note about School Boards and Their Policy-Making Challenges

Kirst commented on the evolution of the school board and stated: "A strange animal, the school board. It must create long-range policies, solve short-term crises, juggle federal and state mandates, and satisfy shifting conditions of teachers, students, community residents, and reformers of every stripe. It receives little praise and accepts great blame for not giving society the education it expects—even when society is not sure what it does want" (Kirst, 1991, p. 1). Presently, school boards are faced with diverse and changing coalitions from within and without the school system.

HOW SCHOOL POLICIES ARE INITIATED

School board policies are initiated in a variety of ways.

- The general deliberations of the school board often result in fostering policy needs.
- Recommendations from the school superintendent often lead to new policies.
- Recommendations from site-based councils often call for policy development.
- Current problems being encountered within the school district tend to bring about policy needs.
- Effective program planning by school leaders at the local level will initiate policy activity.
- Negotiations with teacher and/or support staff associations will initiate "required" policy considerations.
- Lay groups and parent/teacher associations point out needs for policy development or revision.
- Federal and state legislative rulings often require statutory policies for schools.
- Court rulings commonly hold implications for required educational policies.
- State and national school board associations commonly recommend policy development.

The department of education in most states has set forth advice on the policies and documents that governing bodies and proprietors of schools are required to have by law. For example, one section of statutory policies required by education legislation in one state included capability of staff, charging and remissions, school behavior, sex education, special education needs, teacher appraisal, and teachers' pay. Data protection and health and safety policies were required by other legislation.

Other statutory documents required seventeen additional policy requirements including freedom of information, admission arrangements, central record of recruitment and vetting checks, complaint procedure statement, equality information and objectives, register of pupil attendance, staff discipline, conduct, grievance procedures, and others. Documents referenced in statutory guidance included child protection policy and procedures, procedures for dealing with allegations of abuse, and supporting pupils with medical conditions. We view policy adoption as an authority given only to the school board by the state legislature. However, the foregoing information illustrates the major involvement of state/federal influences.

The increasing scope of state and federal involvement in educational actions has standardized such factors as instructional policy and standards that must be met. The school board's discretion regarding policy decision has been reduced by increasing regulations from the state legislatures. Special interest groups and professional councils and commissions have increased their influence on school academic standards and local decision making. The topic of local control relative to policy development is discussed in depth in chapter 3.

School districts are less able to control their own destiny with increasing state and federal controls. Indicating that school boards must assume more responsibility for implementing effective policy measures locally is, of course, a simplification of the situation at hand. Most everyone would agree that those persons who will be affected by governance policies and regulations should be able to participate in their development. Individuals tend to support what they help create.

School boards can only become stronger by building on the fact that they still have strong support of the American public. In an early study of the status of school boards, the public viewed school boards as serving to maintain a close relationship with the citizenry and inhibiting the increase of control by others such as state and federal authorities (Kirst, 1991). Some argue that school boards must do much more to eliminate the apathy that is revealed in the lack of knowledge regarding their role and responsibilities. In addition, school boards have been viewed as being distant from other civic and political mainstream decision-making bodies.

THE UNDERLYING CONCERN: LOCAL CONTROL OF EDUCATION

Figure 1.2, presented previously, was viewed as a conceptual model of policy development. The term "conceptual" was used due to the fact that policy development in education is seldom initiated at the local school level. It is clear that the NSBA and its related state associations describe the policies for school districts nationally. It is a common practice for the NSBA or a state school board association to draft a policy that is derived from a state or federal law or court ruling.

One member of a state's school board stated, "We believe in local control." The member viewed local control as when the school board association drafts a policy and sends it to the state's local school boards, that the local school board has the option of adopting the policy or not. Of course, the local board had the ability to revise the policy if it so desired. This procedure is not local control as we view the process. The same member reported that 99 percent of the state's school districts used the policy system of the state school board. As one would conclude, most every school district in the state has the same school policies and regulations.

Small turnouts for school elections, bond issues, budget overrides, and parent-teacher events reflect apathy and a lack of knowledge about the basic instrumental importance of school board functions. Few persons are aware of the importance of education for preserving a democratic form of government, supporting America's free enterprise economic system, and, as Abraham Lincoln stated, giving each individual a good start and fair chance in the race of life.

How much has been discussed in recent political elections about supporting and providing needed resources for education in America? In the latest national presidential election, about all we heard was that we need to improve education in our schools and we need to provide a free college education for all students; in-depth, comprehensive educational improvement plans were missing.

WHAT NEEDS TO BE DONE? THE STUDY AND REVISION OF THE DISTRICT'S POLICIES AND REGULATIONS

Developing and/or revising the school district's policies and regulations are major tasks. Nevertheless, the benefits of doing so are more than worth the effort needed to accomplish them. It seems wise to approach the tasks in an orderly fashion and deal with only one section of the policy series at a time. A school district policy manual is not required by law in all states. Nevertheless, having a policy manual and keeping it up to date augers well for the prudent operation of the school district. Formatting and organizing the policy manual so that it is easy to use is crucial. Experience suggests several ways in which usability is enhanced:

1. If possible, keep school district policies and administrative regulations readily available electronically. Policy additions are quite easily inserted electronically in their proper place in the manual. Some schools make the policy/regulation manual available on computers placed in the employees' lounge. In the case of printed manuals, use a loose-leaf notebook to make policies easy to catalog, access, and review.
2. Include a table of contents and an index to expedite the location of policy contents.
3. Use the Davies-Brickell or NSBA systems for codification purposes, but change or add major series to meet the conditions of your school district.
4. Be sure to date each adopted policy and dates of policy changes. Use other citations to address such information as crossover entries, relation to state statutes/rules or federal laws/mandates, and court rulings. It is important for the school superintendent to keep ahead of the nation, state, and school district's educational problems and issues.
5. Arrange for easy access to the policies and policy/regulation additions/ changes on the part of parents and other school community members. We recommend that appropriate steps be taken to make the policy manual available to students as well, although a student personnel handbook is a common source for certain policy information (i.e., Section J—students or Section 5000—students). Be certain to establish awareness strategies for keeping the staff, students, and parents informed.

ON YOUR MARK, GET SET, GO

School board policy development can be initiated in several ways. The leadership and recommendations of the school superintendent are important. Minutes of past school board meetings can reveal potential policy needs. Suggestions and problems of various school and citizen committees might prompt policy needs. Results of work on the school district's mission and vision statements most likely suggest policy provisions. Employee grievance reports and negotiations commonly uncover problem areas needing policy clarification. Oft-occurring issues and problems encountered by the school board lend evidence that directive policies are in order, and program evaluation and assessment results commonly hold implications for purpose and procedural direction.

Norton (2008) recommended ten steps for accomplishing the task at hand:

Step 1. Examine various school and community documents and resources for information relative to what policy decisions already have been determined. Include such sources as school board minutes and correspondence, board and staff committee reports, newspaper files, state statutes and federal mandates, and legal documents related to school district activities.

Step 2. Check on established practices in educational administration and operations of former school boards that often reflect embedded practices that imply policy need areas. Unwritten policies are often the basis for newly written policies for current goals and objectives.

Step 3. Investigate what other school boards have done in the development of school policy. Such information can serve as a guide to possible policy development rather than being directly applicable to the local district in question.

Step 4. Examine the minutes of the past school board meetings to determine what intended policies might already have been determined. The school policy manuals, handbooks, and policy writings of other school boards and state and national school boards associations will give clues to important policy topics that have implications for the school district.

Step 5. Enlist the aid of all concerned including citizen groups and educational personnel from other school districts. Such involvement is conducive to quality results.

Step 6. Organize study groups to examine policy needs and to participate in helping perform the related tasks recommended in steps 1 through 5. Establish a steering committee consisting of the most knowledgeable persons to serve as a liaison with study groups in checking for consistency in the policies suggested.

Step 7. Have the school superintendent and administrative cabinet review the policy work completed.

Step 8. Have the school board review the "completed" policy work. The board as a whole should review the semifinal policy drafts and make recommendations for revision.

Step 9. Having the policies examined for compliance with legal statutes helps to build school board and district confidence and lends support to the final policy package.

Step 10. Use first and second readings of the personnel policy statements prior to official adoption. School board policy is legally binding for all school personnel and thus is a contract between the school board and its personnel.

UNDERSCORING FIVE SIGNIFICANT CAVEATS

All chapters of the book make it of primary importance to understand several caveats that affect the development and codification of school board policies and administrative regulations. These five caveats are important for you to keep in mind.

1. The Davies-Brickell system and the NSBA system are foundational for virtually every school policy system in operation at the local school level nationally. However, the series headings within these systems have changed to some extent over the years. For example, the section of *negotiations* might be changed in some cases to professional negotiations or to meet and confer. Section L of the NSBA policies has changed from Interorganizational Relations to such headings as Educational Agency Relations.
2. A specific NSBA policy and and/or regulation that might be included in the policy manual of one school district might not be included in another district. When this occurs, the headings for a code such as GABE will be different.
3. Keeping the school district's policy manual up to date is of primary importance. Even though two school districts might use the same state's policy service, failure to update the policy manual in one district inhibits the use of such services provided by a policy index.
4. Most every school district's policy manual is now online for anyone to examine. The positive outcomes of this practice center around the feeling of openness on the part of the school district board and administration and time that is saved by eliminating the need of school personnel to answer a patron's policy questions personally. On the other hand, we know of no studies that have been done to learn to what extent the Web is used on the part of citizens or school staff to visit the Web on policy matters. Although the procedure tends to influence the time spent by school personnel on the dissemination/explanation of policy, it also reduces important patron/school communication.
5. If we can accept the statement of William E. Dickinson (1970), former member of the National School Boards Association, that "written and continuously updated policies are the sine qua non of a soundly organized and efficiently operated school," then school boards of America need to pay more attention to demonstrating leadership and cooperative policy development of board, administrative personnel, teachers, students, and the citizenry. Chapter 4 deals more in depth with this contention. Local control cannot be viewed as having state school boards draft the school district's educational policies and the board simply approve them. This practice violates every tenet of local leadership, local control, and community cultural sanctions.

POST-QUIZ ON POLICY

Check each of the following true or false questions. Check your score at the end of the quiz.

1. A policy answers the question of "What to do." ____T or ____F
2. Policies are executive in nature. ____T or ____F
3. Only the school can adopt official school board policies. ____T or ____F
4. Policies are developed through board action with administrative leadership. ____T or ____F
5. One criterion of a policy is that it tends to be applicable over long periods of time. ____T or ____F
6. A bylaw is a statement, developed by the professional staff, to supplement an unclear policy originally adopted by the board. ____T or ____F
7. One of the biggest helps the school board receives from policy making is more freedom. ____T or ____F
8. Policy making is considered a project as opposed to a process. ____T or ____F
9. Administrative regulations, although considered to be the responsibility of the superintendent and professional staff, are legally under the authority of the school board. ____T or ____F
10. In regard to policy content, an actual state, federal, or court law should never be included in the school district's policy manual. ____T or ____F
11. An administrative regulation is related to the question of "How to do." ____T or ____F
12. One of the greatest benefits to the school superintendent and professional staff of effective administrative regulations is freedom to administer. ____T or ____F
13. Best estimates would conclude that 95 percent of the nation's school boards have an effective system of policy development in place. ____T or ____F
14. The statement "The school buildings and facilities shall be made available for citizen use within the limits of the law, and insofar as such usage does not conflict with the instructional programs and activity programs of the school" is an administrative regulation. ____T or ____F
15. "No smoking in this school or on the school property of this school" has the characteristics of a school policy. ____T or ____F

Answers to the Post-Quiz

The answer to #1 is True; #2 is False; #3 is True; #4 is True; #5 is True; #6 is False; #7 is False; #8 is False; #9 is True; #10 is False; #11 is True; #12 is True; #13 is False; #14 is False; #15 is False.

Scoring Results

    15 to 13 correct *****
    12 to 10 correct ****
    9 to 7 correct ***
    6 to 4 correct **
    3 to 1 correct *
    0 correct (Begin homework assignment starting on p. 1)

KEY CHAPTER IDEAS AND RECOMMENDATIONS

- Professional knowledge and effective skills related to policy and regulation development are important in meeting a school district's goals and objectives. The vocabulary used in relation to education policy, regulations, and bylaws is as important to education as specific terminology serves professions such as medicine and law. Incorrect definitions of policy, regulations, bylaws, and rules inhibit the effectiveness of educational governance. Such terms commonly are used incorrectly by educators in schools today.
- Policy development on the part of school boards nationally is still lacking in a high percentage of school districts. School board and administrative leadership must be greatly improved in the area of policy development if local control of education is to be realized.
- School boards are legislative bodies and the only ones that can approve school policy. Thus, school board members must be knowledgeable and skilled in policy development, the reason for which they are elected to the position.
- In order to be effective in policy development, school board members must work to overcome the factors that have inhibited the process. The lack of administrative leadership and knowledge of how to do the task has led to policy controls by external agencies and associations.
- Everyone benefits by having a viable system of policy development. The school board benefits by having the control that it wants, and the school administration benefits by being given the discretion to implement policies administratively.
- Educational goals are developed according to the cultural sanctions of the school community and the lay and professional judgments of the community. School policies are ultimately determined by the cultural sanctions of the school community and lay/professional judgments. In turn, the administrative personnel and professional staff develop procedures to implement the school board's adopted policies.

A Pathway to Effective Policy and Administrative Regulation Development 23

- Policy classifications/codification models are readily available to help school districts use policies and regulations effectively. The work of the National School Boards Association and Davies-Brickell laid important foundations for codifying and using school policies and recommendations.
- Involvement in the policy-making process is of prime importance. People tend to support programs and school processes in which they have been involved.
- Difficult tasks such as policy and regulation development take much time and effort. Models for implementing a policy system are available. Research, cooperative programming, and working to develop one policy series at a time are advisable.
- Educators and the public must be given an opportunity to understand the vital importance of policy development in promoting quality education in the school district. Teachers and local administrators have demonstrated little interest in school board policy development and therefore have little interest, know-how, or commitment to governance documents. Many national school districts have yet to implement an effective system of policy and regulation development.
- The incorrect definitions of governance terms in education tend to confuse and inhibit progress for effective policy development at the local school level.

DISCUSSION QUESTIONS

1. Turn back to the opening chapter statement regarding the major chapter goal of defining and illustrating the basic terms of educational governance. Review the terms of district policy, administrative regulations, school board bylaws, school rules, state and federal laws, and the importance of governance policies in promoting educational goals and objectives. To what extent did chapter 1 serve this goal? Name several key ideas in the chapter that were most informative for you. Keep in mind that chapter 2 will focus on the application of policy and regulation codification methods.
2. Assume that you are serving as a school principal. You are addressing your school personnel at the first meeting of the year. Of the forty-two certificated and noncertificated staff personnel in your school, five are new to teaching and four are new classified personnel. The school superintendent has asked school principals to include the item of school policy and regulations in the agenda of staff meetings. Time is limited. Nevertheless, write out how you would handle and address the policy/regulation topic at the meeting.

3. You are the school principal and presiding at a meeting of the school staff. The topic of administrative regulations is raised by one teacher who states that school board policies just restrict our autonomy and give us less freedom to use our own initiative. How will you respond?
4. Chapter 1 submits that school board policies are, in part, local adaptations of education goals developed through cultural sanctions, professional judgments, and lay judgments. Just what does this statement mean? How is the statement best interpreted?
5. Explain your experience with policy and regulation development in school districts as a teacher, administrator, or perhaps a parent in a school district. Give thought to your involvement in policy development activities. To what extent have school policy and/or administrative regulations been present in your work life? How important or unimportant has the topic been for you personally?
6. Why should the school board review and improve the administrative regulations developed by the school superintendent and professional staff?
7. Explain the statement that "the school board gains the control it needs" by having a viable set of governance policies.

CASE STUDIES

Case Study 1—Is a School Board Bylaw Needed Regarding Quid Pro Quo Treatment?

All five members of the Wymore School Board in Lafayette were scheduled to attend the annual school board conference in Las Vegas, Nevada. It was a traditional practice for all board member expenses for the conference trip to be paid from the school district's staff development budget. The wives of the board members were to accompany their husbands to Las Vegas, but their expenses were to be paid by the Chase Moving Company located within the school district of Lafayette. The wives did plan to attend the entertainment programs sponsored by the conference, but their primary interest was the atmosphere and activities that take place in the environment of Las Vegas.

The school board members talked about the conference and its educational value along with the opportunity to meet and discuss common programs and school board issues. In addition, board president Tim Korner spoke of the benefits of board members socializing in a relaxed atmosphere and fostering a friendly relationship in working together. As one board member stated, "One doesn't go to conferences to make policy and pass resolutions. Just the benefits of attending the conference was much more important than trying to justify travel costs and related expenses."

The local newspaper, the *Wymore Tribune*, however, included a piece in the editorial column questioning the wisdom of having the entire school board absent from the community for one full week. In addition, the paper pointed out that the board had turned down funds for the high school's band to travel to the state capital for its annual band day at the university football game.

After the Las Vegas trip, the Wymore Teachers Association sent a letter to the newspaper questioning the large expense of the board members' trip and the fact that the staff development budget for staff and classified personnel had been cut by 15 percent, leaving fewer opportunities for school personnel to travel. Following that letter to the editor, other letters sent to the newspaper were both positive and negative. For example, one patron commented that one board member could have brought back any important knowledge/information from the conference; it doesn't take all five to do so.

Another noted that the school district's board members worked for free and deserved support for all of the time and effort they give to the community. Still another patron questioned the practice of using travel money from a local business or other external party to defray personal board member expenses—in this case attendance by the members' wives.

Discussion Questions

1. What appears to be needed to take care of these kinds of board activities in the future?
2. If the state has no directives regarding matters such as school board travel and conference attendance, might a school board policy or bylaw be drafted on the matter, disseminated appropriately, and then presented for board adoption? Your opinion.
3. Discuss the situation whereby a community business was paying the expenses of the school board members' wives for the Las Vegas trip. How might such matters be resolved in the future before they become school board problems?

Case Study 2—A Matter of Moral Violation

The Mayfair School District had focused on student personnel policy all during the previous school year. The school board was especially concerned with matters of student personnel that centered on school disruption, code of conduct, and school attendance while pregnant. In brief, the school board approved a policy that authorized the local school principal and school nurse to determine school attendance in cases of student pregnancy. In turn, the school superintendent developed an administrative regulation that delegated this responsibility to the local school principal and school nurse.

Nancy Richard was a junior at Mayfair High School and in her fifth month of pregnancy. The school principal drafted a school rule to the effect that student pregnancy of single or married students was contrary to the environment of Mayfair High School and therefore a pregnant student was ineligible to attend the school but would be afforded the opportunity of the home schooling program.

Nancy Richard's mother sought legal help on this matter, insisting that it was her daughter's legal right to attend high school classes on site and stated that her daughter's physician had approved continued attendance in school.

Case Study Discussion

The legal counsel of Nancy Richard's mother turned to the case of Holt v. Shelton (341, F. Supp. 821 [M. D. Tenn. 1972]) (Norton, 2016). The court ruled that when an expectant mother's physician approved continued attendance in school, pregnant students are permitted to continue school in all instances.

In 2013, the U.S. Department of Education published a comprehensive report on the topic, *Supporting the Academic Success of Pregnant and Parenting Students*. The excellent publication presents a comprehensive report of the provisions for pregnant and parenting students under Title IX of the Education Amendments of 1972.

The publication answers such questions as: (1) May a school require a pregnant student to participate in a separate program for pregnant students? (2) What types of assistance must a school provide a pregnant student at school? (3) What if some teachers at a school have their own class attendance and make-up work? (4) In addition to allowing a pregnant student to attend classes, does a school need to allow her to participate in school clubs, class activities, interscholastic sports, and other school-sponsored organizations?

The answer to question #1 is No. Any such requirement would violate Title IX. Regarding question #2, a school must make adjustments to the regular program that are reasonable and responsive to the student's temporary pregnancy needs. Relative to question #3, schools must ensure that the policies and practices of individual teachers do not discriminate against pregnant students. The answer to question #5 is clear. Title IX prohibits a school from excluding a pregnant student from any part of its educational program, including all extracurricular activities, such as school clubs, academic societies, honors programs, homecoming court, or interscholastic sports.

One can readily see the necessity and opportunity for the school district to devise official school board policies and administrative regulations for this one section of student services. Pregnant students do not lose their rights and privileges to receive a public education. In addition, they may take part in the school's extracurricular activities unless a physician sets forth a reason why the student should not do so (Norton, 2016).

Case 2 is an example of a school district's rules being invalid due to a superior court's ruling. In no instance can a school rule, administrative regulation, or school board policy be contrary to a higher court ruling or legislative statute or federal law.

REFERENCES

Arkansas School Boards Association (2015). *Model policies.* Little Rock, AR.

Davies, D. R., & Brickell, H. M. (1958). *An instructional handbook on how to develop school board policies, by-laws, and administrative regulations.* Naco, AZ: Daniel R. Davies.

Dickinson, W. E. (1970, February 28). Development of a school board policy codification system and school board policy information clearinghouse, National School Boards Association, Evanston, IL. Project No. 9-0179, U.S. Department of Health, Education, and Welfare. Office of Education, Bureau of Research, Washington, DC.

Dwight Public Schools #230 & 232 (undated). *School board: Board policy development.* Dwight, IL: Author.

Hunter, F. (1953). *Community power structure.* Chapel Hill: University of North Carolina Press.

Kirst, M. K. (1991, November). School board: Evolution of an American institution. *The American School Board Journal.*

Meador, D. (2016, January 17). Drafting meaningful and effective policies and regulations. *About Education,* teaching.about.com/od/admin/a/Writing-School-Policies--and-Procedures.htm.

Norton, M. S. (2008). *Human resources administration for educational leaders.* Thousand Oaks, CA: Sage.

———. (2016). *The legal world of the school principal: What leaders need to know about school law.* Lanham, MD: Rowman & Littlefield.

Rich, J. M. (1974). *New directions in educational policy.* Lincoln, NE: Professional Educators Publications.

Wikipedia (2016, October). *Dewey decimal classification,* http://en.wikipedia.org/wiki/Dewey_Decimal_Classification.

Chapter 2

Effective Use

Putting the School Policies and Regulations to Work

Primary Chapter Goal: To set forth the process of classifying school policies and regulations and developing the knowledge and skills of school personnel for fostering the ability to use these governance documents effectively.

HOW TO CODIFY SCHOOL POLICIES AND ADMINISTRATIVE REGULATIONS

It was noted in chapter 1 that trying to organize books in a public library without the use of the Dewey Decimal System would be troublesome at best. Librarians use the Dewey Decimal System to organize books according to ten specific classifications:

000—General Works, Computer Science, and Information
100—Philosophy and Psychology
200—Religion
300—Social Sciences
400—Language
500—Pure Science
600—Technology
700—Arts and Recreation
800—Literature
900—History and Geography

The Dewey Decimal System is an Arabic classification that has a number for all subjects, although many libraries create a fiction section shelved by alphabetical order of the author's surname (McCarty & Ramsey, 1971).

Each assigned number consists of two parts: a class number (from the Dewey system) and a book number, which prevents confusion of different books on the same subject. For example, a class number 330 for economics, plus .9 for geographic treatment and .04 for periodicals concerning Europe results in the classification number 330.94 for European economy (Wikipedia, 2016, October 26).

We introduce the Dewey Decimal System because of its basic codification relationship to those used for school district policy classifications discussed in the following section.

Two foundational policy codifying systems are used in school districts today: the Davies-Brickell system (1958) and the National School Boards Association system (Dickinson, 1970). These policy systems have characteristics similar to the Dewey Decimal System except that the NSBA system is an Alpha system and it uses letters rather than numbers for coding purposes. Chapter 1 identified nine major sections in the series for the Davies-Brickell classification system.

Whenever the number 4 leads the code entry, it is related to *Personnel* (4000). The number "4" indicates the section of the entry. Other numbers are used to indicate the subsection, division, subdivision, item, and sub-item of the section. For example, the codification number 4121.13 refers to section 4, subsection 1, division 2, subdivision 1, item 1, and sub-item 3. Similarly, the section number 4219.1 refers to section 4, subsection 2, division 1, subdivision 9, and item 1.

The Davies-Brickell system commonly has three subsections under section 4: Certified Personnel, 4100; Classified Personnel, 4200; and Management and Supervisory Personnel, 4300. Thus, the codification number 4100 would refer to section 4 personnel, and subsection 1 would refer to certificated personnel. The division headings for certified and classified personnel are lengthy.

Sometimes the entries for subdivisions have more than nine entries, which poses a problem for the Davies-Brickell system. For example, how could one deal with a section or division that had more than nine entries? Only up to

Table 2.1

Community Relations	1000
Administration	2000
Business and Noninstructional Operations	3000
Personnel	4000
Students	5000
Instruction	6000
New Construction	7000
Internal Board Policies	8000
Bylaws	9000

nine entries are possible. If the number 10 were to be inserted in any code number, it would skew the reading incorrectly. For instance, in the example in the foregoing paragraph, consider the code number 4219.1. One can see the difficulty of trying to enter the number 10 for any of the digits in the code. The NSBA policy system obviates this problem because it uses letters, and the alphabet has twenty-six of them. In addition, the Alpha system does not use decimal points. Those persons who favor the NSBA system contend that having no decimals reduces the probability of errors in printing and filing.

We make every effort toward having this book be reader friendly. In the case of chapter 2, however, just reading the content might not prove satisfactory. Becoming skilled in policy and regulation codification systems requires studying the contents and working the exercises set forth for the purpose of engaging in the process and learning the methods that accompany policy development. When you study and then complete the work exercises provided in the chapter, you will gain the knowledge and skill of policy and regulation development to become a respected counsel for policy development in your school district.

POLICY GOVERNANCE IS A PROCESS, NOT A PROJECT!

The Davies-Brickell classification series set forth in the foregoing discussion included section 6000, Instruction. Section 6000 of the Davies-Brickell contains five divisions within subsection 6100 with the heading of Elementary and Secondary. The five divisions are A. Schedules, code 6110; B. Objectives of the Instructional Program, code 6120; C. Organizational Plans, code 6130; D. Curriculum, code 6140; and Instructional Arrangements, code 6150.

Consider the five entries under the division Schedules in table 2.2. The code number for Schedules as noted in table 2.2 is 6110. The number 6 is the section, and the first number 1 is the subsection. The next number 1 is the division. At present, 6110 shows no subdivisions. Let's add the four subdivisions. The number 6111 adds the subdivision of School Calendar; 6112 adds the subdivision of School Day; 6113 adds the subdivision of Released Time; and 6114 adds the subdivision of Emergencies.

Policy and regulation development in education is viewed as a process as opposed to a project. The ongoing changes that occur in education make it necessary to revise, add, and delete policies and regulations. Although the topical headings for school policies are derived from a variety of sources, the most viable policies and regulations evolve from the vision and needs of the local school district. Because policies are general statements of school board decisions, principles, and courses of action aimed at the achievement of stated goals, ideally they evolve from local school community initiatives (Norton, 2008).

An interesting note is the increase in policy development from 1999 to 2016 in one school district in Arizona. In 1999, when the present superintendent took office, the school district's policy manual consumed 529 pages. In his seventeen years in the position, the policy manual more than doubled to 1,079 pages. Of course, the increase in federal mandates and state statutes had a great deal to do with the policy increases, but local concerns were a large part of the policy increases as well. Indeed, policy development is a continuous process.

Table 2.2   Section 6000, Instruction. Davies-Brickell Policy Codification System

1. Elementary and Secondary	6100
A. Schedules	6110
1. School Calendar	6111
2. School Day	6112
a. Time Allotments	6112.1
3. Released Time	6113
a. Special Instruction for Students	6113.1
b. Special Activities for Teachers	6113.2
4. Emergencies	6114
a. Fire	6114.1
b. Civil Defense	6114.2
c. Bomb Threats	6114.3
d. Tornadoes and Hurricanes	6114.4
e. Enemy Attack	6114.5
f. Inclement Weather	6114.6
5. Ceremonies and Observances	6115
B. Objectives of the Instructional Program	6120
C. Organizational Plans	6130
D. Curriculum	6140
1. Curriculum Design	6141
a. Experimental/Innovative Programs	6141.1
(i) Sex Education	6141.11
b. Recognition of Religious Beliefs and Customs	6141.2
c. Local Adaptions	6141.3
2. Subject Fields	6142
3. Curriculum Guides	6143
4. Controversial Issues	6144
a. Student Freedom	6144.1
5. Extra-Class Activities	6145
a. Intramural Activities	6145.1
b. Interscholastic Athletics	6145.2
c. Publications	6145.3
d. Public Performance	6145.4
e. Organizations: Councils, Cabinets, Committees, Class Activities	6145.5
f. Travel and Exchange Programs	6146.6
E. Instructional Arrangements	6150

Source: Daniel Davies and Henry Brickell, *An Instructional Handbook on How to Develop School Board Policies, Bylaws, and Administrative Regulations* (1988). Reprinted by permission of Daniel Davies, Naco, AZ.

Effective Use 33

A KNOWLEDGE CHECK

Use table 2.2 to answer the following codification questions.

1. Assume that you wanted to add another subsection, Achievement Standards, to the 6000 Instruction section. What number would be used for this entry, and how would the subsection of Achievement Standards be coded? Number for its entry_____ Code Number_____
2. Assume that you wanted to add Special Education to the item of Experimental and Innovative Programs. What would be its entry number and its code number? Number for its entry____ Code Number_____
3. Assume that you wanted to add another emergency, Unauthorized Classroom Intruder, to the Emergencies list. How would it be coded? _____
4. Under code 6130, Organizational Plans, add the subdivision Cooperative Planning and code it. _____
5. Suppose that an entirely new subsection were to be added to the section 6000. Its entry letter would be _____ and its code number would be_____.

Answers to the Knowledge Check

1. Number for its entry would be 2. Code Number would be 6200. Achievement Standards would be the second subsection for the major section, 6000. The first major section was Elementary and Secondary, code 6100.
2. The entry number for the addition would be (2), and the code number would be 6141.12. Code 6141.1 is for Experimental/Innovative Programs, and the addition of Special Education is the second sub-item. The first sub-item was Sex Education (6141.11).
3. The addition of Unauthorized Classroom Intruder would be coded 6114.7. It is the seventh item in the listing.
4. The addition of Cooperative Planning would be coded 6131. It is the first subdivision for the Organizational Plans division.
5. The entry letter for the new subsection would be F. Its code would be 6160. The addition is under the section Instruction; the first subsection, Elementary and Secondary; and is the sixth division of the division.

SERIES 4000 OF THE DAVIES-BRICKELL POLICY CODIFICATION SYSTEM

Previously in the chapter we listed the nine major sections of the Davies-Brickell codification series for school board policies. It is beyond the scope and purposes of the book to list the entire nine entries of the series. For informational and instructional purposes, however, we are listing the entire entries for the personnel series. The listing will serve several purposes. We will be referring to this listing through the remainder of chapter 2 and in the other chapters of the book.

Itemizing just one section will illustrate the comprehensiveness of school policies. It will add to your understanding of the numbering method used in the Davies-Brickell codification system. The several pages of headings set forth for just one section of the series also demonstrate the expansion of a policy manual when the content is included for each section, subsection, division, subdivision, item, and sub-item.

Both the Davies-Brickell and the NSBA policy systems have served school districts for nearly sixty years. However, both systems have been altered by school districts to meet their particular organization situations and needs. In doing so, a school district might add or change the headings used in the policy series for the sections, subsections, divisions, subdivisions, and items.

For example, the Columbia Heights Public Schools in Minnesota uses similar but also different major policy headings. In addition, the sections are numbered 100, 200, 300, up to 900. The student section is numbered 400 and then continues the subsections, divisions, and subdivisions as 401, 402, 403, 404, up to 422 and 422.1. Nevertheless, the two systems, Davies-Brickell and NSBA, mentioned remain foundational to virtually every system set forth by school districts nationally.

THE DAVIES-BRICKELL SYSTEM OF SCHOOL BOARD POLICY MAKING AND ADMINISTRATION

Again, we are not including complete details of each of the nine sections in the Davies-Brickell policy system series, only one section of the series—personnel—in table 2.3. Chapter 2 uses the information in the personnel section to underscore its design, comprehensive content, and rationale for usability in the local school district. Article 4, Personnel, is a lengthy section. In reading and examining the section, observe closely the use of the numbers regarding section, subsection, division, subdivision, item, and sub-item. For example, note that the code number 4112.2, Certification, represents the fourth section, first subsection, first division, second subdivision, and second item in the personnel listing. Look closely for the codification strategy set forth in Article 4.

Table 2.3 Section 4000, Personnel, of the Davies-Brickell Policy System

Article	Personnel	Series
0.	Concept and Roles in Personnel	4000
	A. Goals and Objectives	4010
1.	Certificated Personnel	4100
	A. Permanent Personnel	4110
	1. Recruitment and Selection	4111
	a. Equal Employment Opportunity	4111.1
	b. Vacancies	4111.2
2.	Appointment and Conditions of Employment	4112
	a. Contract	4112.1
	b. Certification	4112.2
	c. Oaths	4112.3
	d. Health Examinations	4112.4
	e. Security	4112.5
	f. Personnel Records	4112.6
	g. Orientation	4112.7
	h. Nepotism	4112.8
	i. Staff Health & Safety	4112.9
	(1). Communicable Diseases	4112.91
	a. HIV-AIDS	4112.911
3.	Assignment & Transfers	4113
	a. Load/Scheduling/Hours/of Employment	4113.1
	b. Promotion/Demotion	4113.2
	c. Work Year	4113.3
	d. Job Sharing	4113.4
4.	Transfer/Reassignment	4114
5.	Evaluation/Supervision	4115
6.	Probationary/Tenure Status	4116
	a. Seniority	4116.1
7.	Separation/Disciplinary Action	4117
	a. Retirement	4117.1
	b. Resignation	4117.2
	c. Personnel Reduction	4117.3
	d. Dismissal/Suspension	4117.4
	(1) Just Cause	4117.41
	(2) Notice; Hearing	4117.42
	(3) Right of Appeal	4117.4
8.	Rights, Responsibilities and Duties	4118
	a. Civil and Legal Rights	4118.1
	(1) Nondiscrimination	4118.11
	(a) Grievance Procedure Title IX	4118.111
	(2) Freedom of Speech	4118.12
	(3) Conflict of Interest	4118.13
	(4) Harassment	4118.14
	b. Professional Responsibilities	4118.2
	(1) Academic Freedom	4118.21
	(2) Code of Ethics	4118.22
	(3) Conduct of Dress	4118.23
	(a) Smoking, Drinking, Use of Drugs on School Premises	4118.231

(*Continued*)

Table 2.3 Section 4000, Personnel, of the Davies-Brickell Policy System (Continued)

Article	Series
(4) Staff/Student Relations	4118.24
c. Duties	4118.3
B. Temporary and Part-Time Personnel	4120
1. Substitute Teachers	4121
2. Student Teachers/Internships	4122
3. Home Teacher	4123
4. Summer School Teachers	4124
5. Adult Education Teachers	4125
6. Consultants	4126
C. Activities	4130
1. Staff Development	4131
a. Exchange Teaching	4131.1
b. Contributions to Fields of Knowledge	4131.2
c. In-Service Education/Independent Study	4131.3
(1) Tuition Reimbursement	4131.3
d. Visitations; Conferences	4131.4
2. Publication or Creation of Materials	4132
a. Copyrights and Patents	4132.1
3. Travel; Reimbursement	4133
4. Tutoring	4134
5. Organizations/Units	4135
(a) Agreement	4135.1
(1) Recognition	4135.11
(2) Personnel Covered	4135.12
(3) Board/School System Rights	4135.13
(4) Association Rights	4135.14
(5) Saving Clause	4135.15
(6) Work Stoppages	4135.16
(b) Communication Contacts	4315.2
(c) Negotiations/Consultation	4315.3
(d) Grievencies/Complaints/Hearings	4315.4
6. Meetings	4136
7. Soliciting and Selling	4137
8. Non-School Employment	4138
(a) Consulting	4138.1
D. Compensation and Related Benefits	4140
1. Salary Guides	4141
2. Salary Checks and Deductions	4142
a. Social Security Deductions	4142.1
3. Extra Pay for Extra Work	4143
4. Insurance/Health and Welfare Benefits	4144
5. Retirement Compensation	4145
a. Tax Sheltered Annuities	4145.1
6. Employment-Related Accommodations	4146
a. Credit Union	4146.1
b. Gifts/Rewards from Board of Education	4146.2
c. Employee Amenities	4146.3
d. Protective Clothing/Devices	4146.4
e. Professional Library	4145.6

7. Employee Safety	4147
8. Employee Protection	4148
E. Leaves and Vacations	4150
1. Short-Term Leaves	4151
a. Personal Illness and Injury	4151.1
(1) Industrial Accident/Illness	4151.11
b. Family Illness/Quarantine	4151.2
c. Bereavement	4151.3
d. Professional Purposes	4151.4
e. Legal and Civic Duties	4151.5
f. Religious Observances	4151.6
g. Emergency/Personal	4151.7
h. Association	4151.8
i. Military	4151.9
2. Long-Term Leaves	4152
a. Sabbatical	4152.1
b. Professional	4152.2
c. Childbearing/Childrearing	4152.3
d. Military	4152.4
e. Health and Hardship	4152.5
f. Personal	4152.6
g. Political	4152.7
h. Association	4152.8
3. Vacation/Holidays	4153
2. Noncertificated Personnel	4200
A. Permanent Personnel	4210
1. Recruitment and Selection	4211
a. Equal Employment Opportunity	4211.1
b. Vacancies	4211.2
2. Appointment and Conditions of Employment	4212
a. Contract	4212.1
b. Certification or Licensing	4212.2
c. Oaths	4212.3
d. Health Examinations	4212.4
e. Security/Credit Check	4212.5
f. Personal Records	4212.6
g. Orientation	4212.7
h. Nepotism; Husband/Wife Employment	4212.8
3. Assignment	4213
a. Load/Scheduling/Hours of Employment	4213.1
b. Promotion/Demotion	4213.2
c. Work Year	4213.3
4. Transfer/Reassignment	4214
5. Evaluation/Supervision	4215
6. Probationary/Continuing Contract Status	4216
a. Seniority	4216.1
7. Separation/Disciplinary Action	4217
a. Retirement	4217.1
b. Resignation	4217.2
c. Layoff/Rehire	4217.3

(Continued)

Table 2.3 Section 4000, Personnel, of the Davies-Brickell Policy System (Continued)

Article — Personnel	Series
d. Dismissal/Suspension	4217.4
(1) Just Cause	4217.41
(2) Notice; Hearing	4217.42
(3) Right of Appeal	4217.43
8. Rights, Responsibilities and Duties	4218
a. Civil and Legal Rights	4218.1
(1) Nondiscrimination	4218.11
(a) Grievance Procedure—Title IX	4218.111
(2) Freedom of Speech	4218.12
(3) Conflict of Interest	4218.13
(b) Employment Responsibilities	4218.2
(1) Code of Ethics	4218.21
(2) Conduct and Dress	4218.22
(a) Smoking, Drinking, Use of Drugs on School Premises	4218.221
(c) Duties	4218.3
(1) Librarians	4218.31
B. Temporary and Part-Time Personnel	4220
1. Substitutes	4221
2. Teacher Aides/Paraprofessionals	4222
C. Activities	4230
1. Growth in Job Skills	4231
a. Visitations; Conferences	4231.1
2. Publications or Creation of Materials	4232
a. Copyrights and Patents	4232.1
3. Travel; Reimbursement	4233
4. Organizations/Units	4234
a. Agreement	4234.1
(1) Recognition	4234.11
(2) Personnel Covered	4234.12
(3) Board/School System Rights	4234.13
(4) Association Rights	4234.14
(5) Savings Clause	4234.15
(6) Work Stoppages	4234.16
b. Communication Contracts	4234.2
c. Negotiation/Consultation	4234.3
d. Grievances/Complaints/Hearings	4234.4
5. Meetings	4235
6. Soliciting and Selling	4236
7. Non-School Employment	4237
D. Compensation and Related Benefits	4240
1. Salary Guides	4241
2. Salary Checks and Deductions	4242
3. Overtime Pay	4243
4. Insurance/Health and Welfare Benefits	4244
5. Retirement Compensation	4245
a. Tax-Sheltered Annuities	4245.1
6. Employment-Related Accommodations	4246
a. Credit Union	4246.1

b. Gifts/Awards from the Board of Education	4246.2
c. Employee Annuities	4246.3
d. Uniforms, Protective Clothing/Devices	4246.4
7. Employee Safety	4247
8. Employee Protection	4248
E. Leaves and Vacations	4250
1. Short-Term Leaves	4251
a. Personal Illness and Injury	4251.1
(1) Industrial Accident/Illness	4251.11
b. Family Illness/Quarantine	4251.2
c. Bereavement	4251.3
d. Occupational Purposes	4251.4
e. Legal and Civic Duties	4251.5
f. Religious Observance	4251.6
g. Emergency/Personal	4251.7
h. Association	4251.8
i. Military	4251.9
2. Long-Term Leaves	4252
a. Sabbatical	4252.1
b. Professional	4252.2
c. Childbearing/Childrearing	4252.3
d. Military	4252.4
e. Health and Hardship	4252.5
f. Personal	4252.6
g. Political	4252.7
h. Association	4252.8
3. Vacation/Holidays	4253

Source: Used by permission of Daniel R. Davies, Davies-Brickell Associates Ltd., 1958, rev. 1988.

SIGNS AND SYMBOLS USED IN THE SCHOOL BOARD POLICY CODIFICATION AND RETRIEVAL SYSTEM

School codification systems use various signs and symbols to denote a special characteristic of a policy system. For example, the letters SN refer to a scope note statement used when necessary in order to clarify and/or limit the intended us of a descriptor entry in the policy manual such as the following:

Administrative Personnel

SN: For school management and supervisory personnel below district superintendent level. Also, a prefix to a policy code to indicate that the identical term and identical school board policy appear elsewhere in the classification system.
   AFC (Also EBBD) Emergency Closings
   EBBD (Also AFC) Emergency Closings
   A prefix to a parenthetical code indicates that a related term and related school policy appear elsewhere in the classification system.
   JCDAC (Cf. IDBB) Drug Use

IDBB (JCDAC) Drug Use

Some systems use the notation -R as an affix to a code to indicate that the statement it describes is an administrative regulation, not a school board policy.

( )* Parenthetical codes with asterisks (and accompanying terms) are not officially part of the EPS classification system but are included to suggest how the system may be expanded by the user.

(HAHAA)* Recognition of Professional Staff
Negotiating Organization

A CODIFICATION CHECKUP

1. Assume that you want to add new item to the heading of Long-Term Leaves (4252). The heading of the new item is Education. Its code would be _____.
2. In addition, two sub-items relating to Education, Teachers and Administrators, are to be added. The code for the first sub-item, Teachers, would be _____; the code number for the second entry, Administrators, would be _____.
3. Assume that you want to add two new sub-items to the code 4235, Meetings. The first sub-item code would be _____; the second sub-item code would be _____.
4. You want to add two items to the code Vacation/Holidays, 4253. The code for the first item would be _____; the code for the second item would be _____.
5. In the Davies-Brickell policy system, numbers of ____ and above cannot be used for coding.

Answers to Codification Checkup

The answer to #1 is 4252.1. The answers to #2 are 4252.11 and 4252.12. The answers to #3 are 4235.1 and 4235.2. The answers to #4 are 4253.1 and 4253.2. The answer to #5 is 10.

The National School Boards Association's Codification System

As was noted in chapter 1, the Alpha codification system uses a similar procedure but uses letters rather than numbers. The Alpha system is based on the following series of twelve headings:

A—Foundations
B—School Board Governance and Operations

C—General School Administration
D—Fiscal Management
E—Support Services
F—Faculty Development
G—Personnel
H—Negotiations
I—Instructional Program
J—Students
K—School Community Relations
L—Education Agency Relations

As was the case with the Davies-Brickell system whereby any section that starts with the number "4" is related to Personnel, in the Alpha system, any section that starts with the letter "G" is always related to Personnel. For the code GBEBA, G is the section, B is the subsection, E is the division, B is the subdivision, and A is the first item. Similarly, in the code GBEBC, G is the _____; B is the _____; E is the _____; B is the _____; and C is the _____.
If you filled in the blank spaces correctly, your answers would be: section, second subsection, fifth division, second subdivision, and third item.

SECTION G OF THE NSBA POLICY CODIFICATION SYSTEM—PERSONNEL

We include section G, Personnel, of the NSBA policy system in table 2.1 for the purposes of explanation, comprehension, and comparison. In this Alpha system, a cross-reference follows several of the entries. For example, for the Staff-Student Relations entry, GAF, a cross-reference of (JP) is included. This simply means that the topic is also included in section (JP) the tenth subsection and sixteenth division of the policies. Once again, section G is a comprehensive listing. However, the listing will be used additionally in this chapter and the remaining chapters of the book.

FIGURE 2.1: THE NSBA POLICY CODIFICATION SYSTEM-SECTION G—PERSONNEL

- GA—Personnel Policies Goals
- GAA—Staff Time Schedules
- GAB—Responsible Computer System Use (IBEA)

- GAB-R—ACPS Employee Responsible Use Policy Agreement for Computer Systems (Regulation IIBEA-R)
- GAC—Employee Use of Social Media
- GAC-R—Social Media Regulations
- GAD—Access to Employee Social Media Accounts (JHG)
- GAE—Child Abuse and Neglect Reporting (JHG)
- GAE-R—Regulations on Child Abuse and Neglect Reporting (JHG-R)
- GB—Equal Employment Opportunity/Nondiscrimination
- GBA—Sexual Harassment/Harassment Based on Race, National Origin, Disability, Religion, Gender, Gender Identity Gender Expression, and Sexual Orientation (JFHA)
- GB-R/GBA-R—Procedures for Investigating Complaints of Discrimination and Harassment (JFHA-R)
- GBAA—Prevention of Sexual Misconduct and Abuse (JHA)
- GBB—Staff Involvement in Decision Making
- GBD—Board Staff Communication (BG)
- GBE—Staff Health
- GBEA—Unlawful Manufacture, Distribution, Dispensing, Possession, or Use of a Controlled Substance
- GBEB—Staff Weapons in School
- GBEC—Tobacco Free School for Staff and Students (JFCH)
- GBECA—Electronic Cigarettes (JFCHA)
- GBEF—Lactation Support (JHCL)
- GBG—Staff Participation in Political Activities and School Board Election Campaigns (KE)
- GBI—Staff Gifts and Solicitations
- GBL—Personal Records
- GBLA—Third-Party Complaints against Employee
- GBM—Licensed Staff Grievances
- GBM-R—Licensed Staff Grievance Regulations
- GBMA—Support Staff Grievances
- GBMA-R—Support Staff Grievance Regulations
- GBN—Applications for Positions
- GBO—Retirement System
- GC—Licensed Staff
- GCB—Licensed Staff Contracts
- GCBA—Staff Salary Schedules
- GCBB—Supplementary Pay
- GCBC—Staff Fringe Benefits
- GCBD—Staff Leaves and Absences
- GCBD-R—Staff Leaves and Absences Regulations (GDBD)
- GCBE—Family and Medical Leave
- GCBEA—Leave without Pay

- GCBEB—Military Leave and Benefits
- GCCB—Employment of Family Members
- GCDA—Effect of Criminal Conviction
- GCE—Part-Time and Substitute Licensed Staff Employment
- GCG—Professional Staff Probationary Term and Continuing Contract
- GCI—Licensed Staff Assignments and Transfers
- GCI-R—Licensed Staff Assignments and Transfer Regulations
- GCL—Professional Staff Development
- GCN—Evaluation of Licensed Staff
- GCPA—Reduction in Licensed Staff Workforce
- GCPA-R—Reduction in Licensed Staff Workforce Regulations
- GCPB—Resignation of Staff Members
- GCPD—Licensed Staff Discipline
- GCPF—Suspension of Staff Members
- GCQA—Non-School Employment by Staff Members
- GCQB—Staff Research and Publishing
- GCQAB—Tutoring for Pay
- GD—Support Staff
- GDB—Support Staff Employment Status
- GDG—Support Staff Probationary Status
- DGI—Support Staff Assignments and Transfers
- GDN—Evaluation of Support Staff
- GDQ—School Bus Drivers
- GEA—Acceptance of Electronic Signatures and Records (JOH)

Source: Alexandria City Public Schools (2016), Alexandria, Virginia. Alvin L. Crawley, Superintendent

Consider the following statement and examine its content in relation to the characteristics of a policy and of an administrative regulation. First, determine if the statement is a policy or an administrative regulation. Next, give the statement a heading. Finally, assign an appropriate code.

It is the responsibility of the superintendent of schools and of persons delegated by him to determine the personnel needs of the school district and to locate suitable candidates to recommend for employment to the board.

There shall be no discrimination against any applicant or candidate for employment by reason of race, ethnicity, religion, marital status, sex, age, or national origin.

It shall be the duty of the schools to see that persons nominated for employment shall meet all qualifications established by law and the board for the type of position for which the nomination is recommended.

Insert your decision on the question whether the statement is a policy or an administrative regulation _____. The statement definitely has the characteristics of a policy. It deals with a general area of prime importance; it answers the question of what to do; it is a broad statement that allows for the discretion of the school superintendent and professional staff; and it could exist for a long period of time. In regard to an appropriate policy code, the statement centers on the section of personnel, it deals with the certificated staff, and it focuses on the processes of selection and recruitment.

Take a moment to examine table 2.3 and determine a code number for the policy using the Davies-Brickell system. The policy section is 4, Personnel. It deals with Certificated Personnel, division 1. It centers on Permanent Personnel, subdivision 1, and specifies Selection and Recruitment, subdivision division 1. Thus, the appropriate code number is 4111.

What would be the code for the foregoing statement in the Alpha system? Once again the statement centers on Personnel, Certificated/Licensed Staff, Permanent Personnel, and Selection and Recruitment. In the Alpha system, the section Personnel is identified as letter G; Certificated/Licensed Personnel would be GC; Permanent Personnel would be GCA; and Recruitment and Selection would be GCAA.

A RELATED ADMINISTRATIVE REGULATION: AN EXECUTIVE RESPONSIBILITY

The foregoing school board policy might be accompanied with several administrative regulations that serve to implement the policy. The following regulation is one example.

In the appointment of teachers and other instructional personnel, special consideration is given to professional preparation, teaching experience, and personal characteristics desirable for effective teaching performance. Each applicant for a position will:

1. Complete an official application form and submit an official transcript of college credits.
2. Submit a curriculum vitae that includes a record of teaching and other work experience.
3. Appear for a personal interview upon request.
4. Include three or more references of persons who know directly of your teaching and work experience performance.
5. Submit evidence that the required state certification for the position in question has been met.
6. Submit other information as requested including a background check that is required by the school board of education.

Effective Use 45

HOW A POLICY/REGULATION INDEX
CAN FACILITATE YOUR WORK

You have found, most likely, that coding school board policies and administrative regulations does take knowledge, skill, time, and understanding. Just locating a topical heading can take time and is sometimes frustrating. The National School Boards Association and the National Education Policy Network (NSBA/NEPN) have created an index that simplifies a policy search. Every policy topical heading has been included in an index to the NEPN Policy Classification System. Each topical heading is listed alphabetically with its related subtopics and specific code letters.

The original index consumes approximately sixty pages of manuscript and thus it is not possible to include it in full in chapter 2. Nevertheless, due to its importance for policy implementation and facilitation of the use of the policy manual, we will include all entries with their codes for one letter of the alphabet, the letter "P." We selected the letter "P" because many of the personnel topics mentioned in this chapter focus on Personnel.

First, however, we illustrate the organization of the index below. This sets forth the index's organization for one page only of alphabet letter "A." The NEPN index for the letter "A" alone is five pages.

Table 2.4 Policy Index Based on the NSBA/NEPN Policy System

Policy Index	
Ability Grouping	IFA
Absences (see Leaves and Absences for types of Leave)	
Administrative Staff Leaves and Absences	GCCB
Instructional Staff Leaves and Absences	GCCA
Professional Staff Leaves and Absences	GCC
Student Absences and Excuses	JH
Support Staff Leaves and Absences	GDC
Abuse of Children (see Child Abuse/Neglect)	
Abusive Language	
Bullying	JICK; IJNDC
Public Conduct on School Property	KFA
Public Participation at Board Meetings	BEDH
Staff Conduct	GBEB
Student Conduct	JIC
Student Publications	JICE
Academic Achievement	JICK; IJNDC
Academic Incentives/Penalties	IKEA
Student Awards, Honors, and Scholarships	JM
Academic Freedom	IB
Acceleration of Students	

(Continued)

Table 2.4 Policy Index Based on the NSBA/NEPN Policy System (Continued)

Policy Index	
Grade Advancement	IKE
Acceleration of At-Risk Students	IHBDC
Acceptable Use of Electronic Resources/Internet	IJNDC
Access to School Buildings	ECAB
Accidents (see also Safety)	
Accident Insurance	
Insurance Program/Risk Management	EI
Worker's Compensation	GBGD
Accident Prevention and Safety Procedures	EBB
Accident Reports	EBBB
Bus Accident/Emergencies	EDAEE
Bus Safety Program	EEAE

It is important to point out that some states have discarded the use of a policy index. First, an index is a lengthy, ever-changing entity. New policies are being added and current policies are being revised and/or dropped continuously. Keeping the index up to date is a tedious task, and often the index is not in order with the new policies being adopted and older policies being cut. State school board associations reportedly find it quite impossible to keep a policy index up to date and in tune with all of the changes in policy development being made by the myriad school districts nationally.

AWARENESS IS IMPORTANT

School policy manuals and the availability of school policies on the Web are important personnel resources found in effective school operations today. In addition, many school district personnel offices have developed handbooks for both classified and certificated personnel to accompany and support the members of the school district's staff. A handbook serves in close relationship to the school district's policy manual.

The Human Resources Department of the Thompson School District of Loveland, Colorado, is one school district that has developed such a handbook for classified personnel. As stated in its introduction, "It is the responsibility of each classified employee to read and become familiar with the contents of this handbook and the Board of Education Policy Book available at all locations."

The Thompson School District's handbook (2006, December) includes nine major content areas of interest: Absences from Work, Benefits, Committee Activity, Evaluation, Operating Practices, Payroll, Safety and Reporting of Injury, Salary Schedule Regulations, and Staff Conduct. The following illustration presents one section of the contents of the handbook that centers on Absences from Work. Partial excerpts from the Absences from Work section are illustrated. Make special note of its references to the school district's policy manual.

CLASSIFIED STAFF PERSONNEL HANDBOOK

Absences from Work

ABSENCES (Ref. Policy GDC)
With the exception of Nutritional Services, Transportation, Administration Building, and Custodial Services, when an employee is absent from work, the employee must notify the Substitute Absence Tracking System prior to his/her regular scheduled start time. Failure to do so may disqualify the employee from using available paid leave. . . . All absences which do not qualify under Board policy (GDBD) are considered unexcused and subject to disciplinary action under the progressive plan.

ANNUAL LEAVE (Reference Policy GDCA/GDCB)
Definition: Annual leave is based on an individual's assignment. Available leave may be used at the professional discretion of the employee for illness or personal business.

A. The district allocates and administrators and/or department supervisors monitor annual leave.
B. Accrued Leave (Ref. Policy ACCR40)
   Definition: Up to 320 hours from annual leave not used in previous years, which may be used for illness only.
C. Available Leave (AN)
   Definition: The total of both accrued and annual leave . . . dependent upon the employee's annual work assignment.
D. Grandfathered Leave Days (GF)
   Definition: Classified employees who have accumulated more than (the required) days by the end of the assigned year can use those days for an extended, long-term illness (personal or an immediate family member) or accident-related injury as verified by a physician's statement.

VACATION (Ref. Policy GDD)
Twelve-month regular classified staff employees are entitled to the following vacation leave:
   First through fourth year of employment ___hours per year
   Fifth through twelfth year of employment ___hours per year
   Thirteenth through each succeeding year ___hours per year

HOLIDAYS (Ref. Policy GDD)
Twelve (12) month classified employees are eligible for 12 paid holidays per year as approved by the Board of Education.

SICK LEAVE BANK
One of your benefits as an . . . employee is the option or participation in the Classified Staff Advisory Council (CSAC) sponsored by the Sick Leave Bank.

DONATE-A-DAY
Donate-A-Day is a way to help employees who need additional day(s) beyond their available days to help a member of their immediate family with a serious illness or injury.

BEREAVEMENT LEAVE (Ref. Policy GDCBC)
Classified staff employees are allowed up to ___hours leave (based on 1.0 FTE) with a full day for a death in the immediate family.

CHILD-CARE LEAVE (Ref. Policy GDCC)
Such a leave may be granted for a period not to exceed one year in addition to the remaining portion of a year during which child-care leave commences.

JURY DUTY (Ref. Policy GDCK)
Employees shall be granted leave with full pay when called to jury duty or subpoenaed to testify as a district employee.

Other Leave Benefits:
MILITARY DUTY (Ref. Policy GDCL)
PERSONAL LEAVE (Red. Policy (GDCBM)
DOMISTIC ABUSE LEAVE (Ref. GBGL)
FAMILY AND MEDICAL LEAVE (Ref. Policy GBGM)

POST-CHAPTER QUIZ

Part 1

1. In the Davies-Brickell Coding System, identify each part of 4142.1 (section, subsection, etc.).
   4th _____ 1st_____
   4th _____ 2nd _____ and 1st
   _____.

2. Identify the topical headings of each entry using figure 4134 and 4211.1 using **table 2.3**.
   A. 4134 is: 4 _____; 1 is _____; 3 _____
   _____; and 4 is _____
   B. 4211.1: _____1; 2 _____;
   1 is _____; 1 is _____
   _____; and 1 is _____

C. If a sub-item were added the item in "B" above, what would be the new code number?
3. Code the following entry using the Davies-Brickell system:
   a. Personnel, Noncertificated Personnel, Leaves and Vacations, Long-Term Leaves; and add a new sub-item of Family Care. Code is _____
   b. Personnel, Certificated Personnel, Permanent Personnel, Assignment and Transfer, Load/Scheduling/Hours/ of Employment: _____
4. Code the following using the NSBA Alpha system.
   a. Personnel, Equal Opportunities/Nondiscrimination, Personal Records
   b. Personnel, Support Staff, Support Staff Employment Status_____
   c. Name each topical entry in the Alpha system for GDN
      G_____
      D_____
      N_____
5. GBO in the Alpha system centers on _____.

Part 2

True or False

_____1. Policy development in the nation's schools was enhanced by the Davies-Brickell and NSBA codification systems when both were established in the early 1980s.
_____2. The NSBA system is the one most widely used for classifying policies and regulations.
_____3. Although some school districts favor the Davies-Brickell system because numbers tend to be easier to use, one potential problem with the system is that any one subsection, division, subdivision, or item is limited to nine entries.
_____4. If another item were added to the code 4233.4, the code would be 4233.41.
_____5. In the Alpha code GCQAB, the letter B is the second sub-item.
_____6. Policy making is considered a project as opposed to a process.
_____7. If a school district is using the policy system of the NSBA, the Alpha code GPA would refer to the section of Personnel. In addition, the subsection and first division headings will be exactly the same for all school districts.
_____8. Administrative regulations are strictly the concern of the administrative staffs of the local school district.
_____9. A policy index serves to assign the code for a new policy adopted by the school board.

_____10. A school district's policy handbooks for certificated and classified staff personnel are excellent substitutes for policy manuals in school districts.

ANSWERS TO THE POST-QUIZ

Part 1

1. Code number 4.142.1 is the fourth section; first subsection; fourth division; second subdivision; and first item.
2. The Davies-Brickell code 4134 is 4 Personnel; 1 Certificated Personnel; 3 Activities; and 4 Tutoring. The code 4211.1 is 4 Personnel; 2 Non-Certificated Personnel; 1 Permanent Personnel; 1 is Recruitment and Selection; and 1 is Equal Employment Opportunity. If a sub-item were added to 4211.1, the code number would be 4211.11.
3. Code in the Davies-Brickell System
   a. Personnel 4, Noncertificated 2, Leaves and Transfers 5, Long-Term Leaves 2, New sub-item Family Care 9. Code 4252.9.
   b. Personnel 4, Certificated Personnel 1, Permanent Personnel 1, Assignment/Transfer/Load/Schedules/Hours/of Employment 1. Code 4113.1.
4. Code in the Alpha System
   a. Personnel G, Equal Opportunity/Nondiscrimination B, Personal Records L: Code GDL.
   b. Personnel G, Support Staff D, Employment Status B: Code GDB.
   c. Personnel G, Support Staff D, Evaluation of Support Staff N: Code GDN.
5. GBO in the Alpha centers on Retirement System.

Part 2

1. False. Both the Davies-Brickell and the National School Boards Association policy systems were initiated by 1958.
2. Probably True. The NSBA continues to provide policy services to school nationally. The Davies-Brickell system, to our knowledge, has no special organization that continues to provide services for schools.
3. True. When more than nine entries are needed in the Davies-Brickell system, the number 10 cannot be used.
4. False. If another item were added to code 4233.4, it would be 4233.5.
5. False. In the code GCQAB, the B is the second item.
6. False. Policy development is definitely a continuing process that must be updated and changed as new entries become necessary.

7. False. GPA could have different topical headings in different school districts. However, the code GPA in any school district's policy manual refers to Personnel, the sixteenth subsection and the first division of the school's manual.
8. False. However, administrative regulations are commonly viewed as being within the jurisdiction of the administrative staff. Nevertheless, such authority for the administration is delegated by the school board that holds legal and legislative authority for administrative regulations as well as school policies.
9. False. A policy index lists the headings for all entries/topics in the policy manual in alphabetical order. It serves much the same purpose as the index of a book.
10. False. An employee handbook can serve to support the policy manual of the school district but is not used to supplant a school's policy manual.

KEY CHAPTER IDEAS AND RECOMMENDATIONS

- Policy and regulation classification systems are similar in methods to the well-known Dewey Decimal System used in libraries. Without such classification systems founded by Davies and Brickell and the National School Boards Association, policy development in education would greatly inhibit effective governance in its operations.
- The classification series used in the Davies-Brickell and NSBA systems are quite similar, but one uses numbers and the other uses letters. Both systems have great benefits including their value in increasing the usability of policies and regulations for educational purposes.
- Gaining an understanding of classification systems requires more than just reading about them. Studying the strategies of codification looms important for gaining the knowledge and skills required for effective policy use.
- Although codification systems have much to offer in the efforts to maintain up-to-date policy manuals in schools, school leaders and school boards must become directly involved in the policy development process; local control of education depends on it.
- Empirical evidence suggests that many school districts in the United States still do not have a system of policy development that lends important operational benefits to all of those concerned about effective education in America.
- The original versions of classifications systems have been adopted by the states but have been changed by school boards to meet the culture and operational needs of their local school communities.

- Effective use of policy manuals and policy statements on the Web depends largely on the school board's and its school personnel's knowledge and skill in its use.
- Electronic policy statements on the Web suggest an open school system. However, the question that needs to be answered is: Can this delivery method be used effectively?
- Involvement may be the most important part of policy and regulation development and implementation. People tend to use and support what they have had a part in developing. Boilerplate policy development and use falls short of assuring the effective use of policy at the local school district level.

DISCUSSION QUESTIONS

1. Give thought to the status of school policies and regulations in your school or to a school that you know best. To what extent, in your opinion, is policy development a matter that is under the control of the state and local school districts? How would you assess the knowledge of the school administration and the school personnel relative to policy development and its importance in operating an effective organization?
2. Assume that you have been assigned the task of working with the certificated and classified personnel in your school relative to policy and regulation development. What information in chapter 2 would you view as of most importance for your remarks?
3. Empirical evidence suggests that school personnel are not adequately prepared to develop viable school policy for school board adoption. What action, in your opinion, is needed to reverse this situation?
4. Chapter 2 focused on the knowledge and skills needed to foster positive policy development in educational systems. On the other hand, school policy commonly is outside the priorities of the large majority of school personnel. As a school leader and professional, why should you be concerned about this situation?
5. What information in chapter 2 was most interesting and/or important, in your opinion? List two or three specific aspects of policy development discussed in chapter 2 that you believe were most helpful to you in your present position.
6. In a meeting of the school board, the topic of student due process hearings was brought to the table. One member states that all the board has to do is ask the state's school board association to send us a policy with related regulations. You are the school superintendent. How will you respond to the school board member's suggestion?

REFERENCES

Alexandria City Public Schools (2016). *School board policy manual*, Section B. Alexandria, VA: Author.

Dickinson, W. E. (1970, February 28). Development of a school board policy codification system and school board policy information clearinghouse, National School Boards Association, Evanston, IL. Project No. 9-0179, U.S. Department of Health, Education, and Welfare. Office of Education, Bureau of Research, Washington, DC.

McCarty, D. J., & Ramsey, C. E. (1971). *The school managers: Dewey decimal system.* Westport, CT: Greenwood.

Norton, M. S. (2008). *Human resources administration for educational leaders.* Thousand Oaks, CA: Sage.

Thompson School District (2006, December). *Classified staff personnel handbook.* Human Resources Department, Loveland, CO: Author.

Wikipedia (2016, October 26). *Dewey decimal classification*, https://en.wikipedia.org/wiki/Dewey_Decimal_Classification.

Wilkinson, W. E., ed. (1970). *Policy system index.* Evanston, IL: National School Boards Association.

Chapter 3

Policy and Regulation Development
The Difference That It Makes

Primary Chapter Goal: To illustrate effective models of exemplary policies and regulations being implemented in school districts nationally and to discuss best practices of school boards, school superintendents, and others in planning, designing, and implementing an effective policy system for optimal operational purposes.

Chapters 1 and 2 focused on the development of an effective policy/regulation system for school districts nationally. We contended that many school districts in the United States have yet to initiate an effective policy development system. Although evidence of local control of policy development is missing in school districts throughout the United States, visits with school superintendents give us substantial evidence that policy development is being handled well in many school districts. To achieve this end, the leadership of the school superintendent is of paramount importance.

Chapter 3 presents applications of effective policy development by school boards and the knowledgeable leadership of school superintendents in assuring a meaningful, relevant, and effective policy program in their schools. Various strategies for assessing the policy system, involving school personnel in policy matters, and monitoring the awareness of the school district's policies are considered in depth in this chapter. Space limitations do not permit the wide dissemination of information and policy forms being used by schools. Nevertheless, we illustrate effective policy practices in place in many school districts and, in doing so, feature exemplary school districts such as the Irvine Unified School District in California and the Mesa School District in Arizona.

INITIATING NEW POLICY: WHOSE RESPONSIBILITY?

"Both logically and valuationally, policy making can be considered the epitome of administrative action—quintessential administration-philosophy-in-action" (Parkinson, 1978, p. 67). Yet, in reality, various studies over the years have revealed that less than 50 percent of school superintendents nationally take the lead in development of policy in their school districts (Norton, 2008).

The adoption of local school policies is regulated commonly by the bylaws of the school board, regulations established by the state's education board, or by state statute. Figure 3.1 sets forth the common procedures for policy adoption in the excellent bylaw illustrated by the Irvine Unified School District of California.

Figure 3.1: POLICY ADOPTION/Local School Policy Adoption   9310
The Board of Education has the primary function of providing policies to guide the actions of those to whom it delegated authority. These policies shall be recorded in writing.

The formulation and adoption of these written policies shall constitute one method by which the Board of Education shall exercise its leadership in the operation of the school system.

In formulating policies, the Board shall adopt general principles and statements of intent. The Superintendent and his/her professional staff shall take action therewith. Application of such policies to individual problems and tasks is an administrative function to be performed by the Superintendent. The Superintendent shall, in turn, when necessary, or when directed by the Board of Education, prepare written regulations to ensure the implementation of Board policy.

The Superintendent, in cooperation with staff and the Board, shall recommend policies for adoption and recommend revision of existing policies. Policies and/or revisions may be proposed by any member of the Board, by any lay group or organization, or by any member of the public.

Specific policy proposals and suggested amendments to or revisions of existing policies shall be submitted to all members of the Board in writing prior to a regularly scheduled Board Meeting. No policy or amendment shall be adopted unless it has been discussed at a meeting prior to adoption, unless a majority of the Board has voted otherwise.

It shall be the duty of the Board to reappraise its policies in view of the changing needs of the community and schools.
Policy Adopted: November 3, 1980
Policy Revised: February 16, 2016

Take special note of the school board bylaw in figure 3.1 relative to the foregoing discussions of policy and regulation definitions. The Irvine Unified

School District makes it clear that its policies are general principles and statements of intent. In addition, the Irvine board has underscored the fact that the application of its policies to individual problems and tasks is an administrative function to be performed by the superintendent. In addition, the school superintendent is to prepare written administrative directions to ensure the implementation of board policy.

THE MATTER OF LOCAL CONTROL: PROS AND CONS

We have favored local control in public schools when the school is being governed and administered by the persons who are most knowledgeable about the interests and needs of the students and because no one is more concerned about the welfare and future of the children and youth in the school community than the school board, parents, administrators, and community members. In order to serve these purposes, local school boards and school leaders must be able to make independent decisions about school goals and objectives and how best to achieve them.

Local control remains a matter of debate. In the next chapter, the primary pros and cons of the ongoing debate are discussed. In any case, when the matter of educational control is debated, the major concern of school finance comes to the floor. That is, in regard to the status of local control, who pays the bill? It is well known that the ability to pay for education differs widely among the states and among school districts within the states. One report indicated that the ability to pay among the states, for example, differed on a scale of 6 to 1. That is, some states are six times more able to pay for educational costs than others. Districts within the various states face the same financial problem. Depending only on local property tax to support the school, of course, is clearly insufficient.

As Chisholm (1953) pointed out more than six decades ago, four factors determine the nature of an acceptable program of school finance: The equitable distribution of the burden of school support among the three levels of government, the local school district or county school system, the state, and the federal government, each level of government assuming responsibility for the support of the schools in proportion to its relative economic strength or basic tax-raising ability.

Best estimates indicate that current public elementary and secondary school financial support is federal, 18.0 percent; state, 45.2 percent; and local, 36.8 percent. Statistical reports tend to differ widely. For example, state per-pupil support for education ranged from $6,546 in Utah to $20,577 in Washington, DC. The per-pupil state annual support exceeded $15,000 in eight states (National Center for Educational Statistics, 2013–2014).

The pros for local control of education include the following contentions:

1. The quality of teaching and learning effectiveness can be improved because the school is administered by the individuals and boards that are most knowledgeable about the school community and its students' interests and needs. As such, administrators, teachers, parents, and community members have a direct interest in the immediate and future success of students who are attending or have attended the local schools.
2. Because school purposes and policy decisions are determined by representative school board members, the governance process includes a close working relationship with members of the community. In turn, community support is fostered.
3. External control is eliminated or substantially reduced, which facilitates positive decision making and implementation of meaningful administrative regulations that can be readily applied to programs for student learning.
4. Some quarters contend that more control of education by the federal and state agencies results in positive outcomes related to closing the gaps in schools in social, finance, and program quality. In fact, some authorities contend that "federal politics and educational policy are inextricably linked" (Lamiell, 2012, February 10, p. 1) with a strong belief that major changes to American schools have resulted from federal law, jurisprudence, or policy. Christopher T. Cross, onetime under secretary of education, was quoted by Lamiell as stating, "The reality is that almost everything that goes on is, in fact, guided by what happened in federal policy at some point, even though people in the classroom may not recognize it" (p. 2).

The cons of local control of education include the following contentions:

1. Controls by the federal government or other external agencies tend to inhibit individual administrator and teacher initiative, especially when such controls mandate what, when, and how certain subjects are to be taught in schools. Such external controls tend to limit community involvement and investment in the school program. External control lessens the degree to which local school board, school leaders, and local schools can govern their schools and make appropriate decisions about school governance important to the school community.
2. Rather than increasing student achievement academically, external control of the school curriculum leads to an emphasis on mandated testing rather than on effective teaching. The lack of teacher autonomy becomes problematic and reportedly increases teacher turnover.

3. Certain external control developments such as school district consolidation commonly result in increases in administrative bureaucracy, student personnel problems, and major emphasis on sports as opposed to academic achievement. Teachers with smaller classes are more able to know the interests and needs of their students than educators in larger school populations.
4. External policy development does not directly evolve from the culture of the local school community. As discussed in chapter 1, policies should be developed on the basis of cultural sanctions and community goals of the local school community. Externally developed policies do not meet this criterion.
5. Some criticism of local control points to bureaucratic red tape that commonly surrounds contradictory views of what's best for education. Standardized curriculum and testing mandates inhibit teacher creativity and militate against attracting creative personnel into the profession of teaching.

LET'S DRAFT A NEW POLICY ON PHASED RETIREMENT

Personnel Retirement: Phased Retirement　　　　　　　　　　　　GBOA
The school board recognizes the value of experienced employees and their contributions to the purposes of the school district. The reemployment of personnel in the Lafayette School District is established to allow more flexibility for more experienced employees to work beyond the present retirement as set forth in policy GBO. Reemployment of classified and certified employees will be based on employee work records as determined by the employee's performance ratings. Reemployment is subject to school district needs and subject to all requirements that may be set forth by state statutes. Reemployment is not guaranteed and is subject to school district needs and position availability. The school superintendent and delegated administrative personnel are responsible for assuring that criteria for reemployment, as determined by state statutes and present school board policy, are met.

The topic of personnel retirement is coded commonly in the Davies/Brickell system as 4117.1. If a new entry were to be added to retirement, such as phased retirement, its code might be 4117.11. In the NSBA codification system, retirement is coded somewhat differently, but GBO is a common code. If a subdivision of phased retirement were added, the code would be GBOA. Although phased retirement might be new to many persons, it has been programmed in some school districts for several years. Phased retirement is any human resources program that allows older workers to reduce their work hours without changing employers and eases the transition to retirement (Employment Policy Foundation, 2003, August 15).

The Employment Policy Foundation lists several reasons for implementing a phased retirement system. According to the foundation, the demand for workers is exceeding the supply. By 2030, for example, the worker shortage will rise to thirty-five million. Several other reasons for phased retirement plans include the fact that

- people are living longer today, and the days in retirement have increased;
- a growing number of persons would like to continue working beyond retirement age;
- both older workers and organizations benefit from phased retirement; workers keep their employment, and the organization keeps the worker talent pool;
- retirees have reported that financial needs have increased since retirement, and additional income is important;
- retirement life styles have not been retained in many cases due to increased living costs and a set retirement income;
- retired persons have had to seek income from work positions outside their personal interests and talents; phased retirement would allow them to continue work in their skill and interest field;
- empirical evidence suggests that persons in a phased retirement plan lead a healthier existence; and
- phased retirement is good for business.

LET'S DRAFT A POLICY ON STUDENT MEDICAL MARIJUANA

The topic of the dispensing of marijuana is at the top of the concerns in various states; it includes marijuana dispensaries and student use of medical marijuana in schools. At the time of this writing, some states had approved the sale of marijuana and others had voted not to do so. Consider the matter of marijuana dispensing from the perspective of members of a school board or the superintendent of schools. What stand might you take on these matters?

As one school superintendent commented, "We're going into some new territory, and we're going to have to work through this. . . . We want to support anyone who needs it for a medical reason, but we have to be very careful with this in a school setting." Reportedly, when one superintendent was asked if any current students were using medical marijuana, he said he was not allowed to comment on that. Another school superintendent said that schools are going back to existing policies and procedures on conduct for student athletes to see if they also need to be changed to recognize student legal rights to use medical marijuana. One superintendent commented that the approval of medical marijuana in schools was not a question of if but when.

Let's assume that you are a school board member or a superintendent of schools. What factors must you consider before acting on a policy for student use of marijuana in your school district? After doing so, we will ask you to draft a proposed policy for consideration of the school board as a whole.

Here are a few of the considerations that must be kept in mind:

- Has the state legislature or state school board of education ruled on the matter of marijuana in the state? If so, what were the specific rulings? In addition, have the courts ruled on marijuana use in the state and/or in the schools specifically?
- Even if the dispensing of medical marijuana has been approved legally in the state, what is the disposition of school parents, members of the school community, and school administrators on the topic of marijuana in the school?
- If the use of medical marijuana is approved by the state and ultimately by the school board, how is it to be dispensed? How is it to be consumed (i.e., edible form, smoking, pharmaceutical medication, vaporization, inhalation, food, liquid drops, injection, or other) and who is authorized to dispense it? If a doctor must approve the student's access to marijuana, does he or she agree to set the conditions of its administration? That is, does the doctor indicate when the "medication" is to be administered and when it is to conclude?
- Is the marijuana to be dispensed by someone in the school or is it to be dispensed by someone outside the school property before or after school? Or can a parent or other primary caregiver dispense marijuana on the school grounds? Is it to be dispensed during or before or after school?
- What written certification/evidence is to be required for a student to be eligible to use marijuana for medical purposes on the school grounds? Where is it to be performed? Is it to be dispensed in the principal's office, the nurse's office if on-site, or elsewhere?
- Who is to assume the possession of the marijuana before and after it is administered?
- Who is to oversee, monitor, and control the entire marijuana process?
- Is there an age limit for students who can be authorized to use medical marijuana in the school?
- What credentials must be submitted by the "caregiver" or individual authorized to administer marijuana on the school site? Will a guardian or caregiver be authorized to assume this role?
- Who stands the responsibility for "medical" problems that might arise, especially when school personnel assume responsibility for administering the doses of marijuana?

WORKSHOP ASSIGNMENT

Have you ever drafted a formal school district policy that ultimately was presented to a committee, school principal, or school superintendent for analysis and assessment? If you have and were successful in doing so, you could decide to skip the following work assignment and move on to reading the remaining sections of the chapter. What is requested here is a learning opportunity for you to draft a policy on student use of marijuana that includes both the characteristics of effective policies and considerations of the questions posed in the foregoing section.

Assume the task seriously by giving thought to the fact that your draft will be reviewed by a school committee, the school superintendent, and perhaps the school district's board. We repeat: you are drafting a policy; administrative regulations will be established later. Avoid reviewing another school's marijuana policy or one that might have been developed by the state school boards association. When your draft is completed, check it with the "model policy draft" set forth a little later in chapter 3.

WHO IS IN CHARGE HERE?

In view of the conflicting views of legalizing marijuana, one has to wonder about the school's authority to control and prohibit the use of tobacco and alcoholic beverages in the school. In fact, nineteen states have approved the use of marijuana for medical purposes; five more states have legalized it for medical and recreational use. Thus, nearly 50 percent of the states have approved the use of marijuana in schools to date.

Most school districts today have policies against the use or possession of drugs or alcohol on the school grounds. Because several states already have approved the use of medical marijuana in schools, districts will need to update their policies as needed. It is yet to be seen whether marijuana use in schools leads to an increase on the part of nonapproved students bringing marijuana and other drugs to the school site.

Presently, "School authorities may control and prohibit the use of tobacco and alcoholic beverages in school" (Peterson, Rossmiller, & Volz, 1978, p. 357). Courts have not questioned school boards' authority to do so. Yet, will the legal rulings on the use of medical marijuana change this perspective? If parents approve, might schools agree to permit students to smoke on school sites if state statutes permit students of a certain age to do so? If smoking is allowed when it does not interfere with the learning of other students, does non-permission violate student rights?

Does the foregoing paragraph appear too ridiculous for you to consider? We are aware of an alternative school—not a charter school—that allows student smoking on the school grounds. Students in the alternative school are ones who have been dismissed from their regular school or dropouts from school who now wish to return to some form of school programming. In any case, whether it be smoking violations or violations with drugs or alcohol, student rights are important.

Peterson and others point out several cases whereby student rights were protected by the courts in cases of drugs and alcohol. The courts have made certain actions by school administrators of considerable importance. For example, in regard to student searches, two criteria loom important:

1. Was the search within the scope of the school official's duties?
2. Was the search reasonable within the facts and circumstances of the case?

The court case of Kelley v. Martin (1971) ruled that a school board may formulate rules and regulations against possession of drugs and expel students for violations, but the constitutional rights of students cannot be violated in doing so. For example, a police officer in school or out is clearly a person who must accord any student searched the full extent of rights guaranteed by the Fourth Amendment.

A POSSIBLE POLICY FOR THE STUDENT USE OF MARIJUANA IN SCHOOL DISTRICTS

The following policy refers back to the matter of student medical marijuana. It includes many of the considerations concerning the approval of use of medical marijuana by students on the school site. Keep in mind that the following example is a policy and not an administrative regulation. Thus, it is designed to meet the definition and characteristics of an effective school board policy; it answers the question of what to do if you drafted a policy as suggested previously in the chapter. Check it with the policy that follows.

4112.8 Student use of medical marijuana
Students within the school district are permitted the use of marijuana for medical purposes in compliance with state statute SS 2017. School officials shall be responsible for verifying the registration status and ongoing authorization concerning the medical use of marijuana for the student and the parent, guardian, or primary caregiver. The Board of Education permits the administration of medical marijuana to a registered student by a registered primary caregiver. School personnel are delegated the responsibility of ensuring that controlled and dangerous substances are not used illegally on school grounds; but the school board authorizes the medical use of marijuana on school grounds, on a school bus, or at a school-sponsored event provided that such use is consistent with legal statutes and the policies of the board. The school board delegates the

responsibility for developing relevant administrative regulations for implementing and monitoring the student use of medical marijuana to the school superintendent and school personnel who are appointed to assist him in assuring an effective implementation of a program for student medical marijuana use in the school.

It is apparent that the work of the school superintendent and staff personnel is of primary importance in developing an effective program plan through relevant and legal administrative regulations. Regulations should be presented to the school board for its input and approval. As you are well aware, the administrative regulations will focus on how the student medical marijuana policy will be implemented and conducted. An examination of the administrative regulations that have been approved by various school districts nationally do have similarities but tend to differ in some respects as well.

For example, some school districts permit only the primary caregiver to administer the marijuana medication; others permit the parent, guardian, and caregiver to do so. Some do not permit the possession or use of medical cannabis on the school bus or on school grounds; others allow the primary caregiver to administer the medication while on the school grounds, aboard a school bus, or while attending a school-sponsored event. In some districts, the use of medical marijuana must have the approval of two doctors rather than one. The method of intake tends to differ among school districts as well; some districts limit intake to edible medical cannabis options rather than smoking or vaporizing.

We underscore the point that the foregoing section is not to set forth administrative procedures as being appropriate for approval, but rather to point out the importance of administrative leadership in determining administrative regulations that serve the appropriate needs of students and meet the statutes set forth by the state in question.

WHAT ABOUT APPROPRIATE ADMINISTRATIVE REGULATIONS?

Reread policy 4112.81 set forth above and then draft several administrative regulations that are appropriate for that policy. Check your regulations with those as follows:

4112.8-R—Students under the age of eighteen, who have a doctor-certified health problem, are eligible to participate in the school district's program to administer medical marijuana that is not administered by smoking or by inhalation. The medical marijuana must be in the hands of the primary caregiver at all times except when another approved individual is involved in the administration process.

4112.82-R—The parent of the student authorized to engage in the medical use of marijuana must submit a written request with supporting documentation to the school principal to have a primary caregiver assist in the administration of medical marijuana to the student while on the school grounds, aboard a school bus, or attending a school-sponsored event.

4112.83-R—The school superintendent is responsible for making sure that the school district's administrative regulations meet the requirements of state and federal law.

4112.84-R—Marijuana medication cannot be stored on school property, and school nurses are not permitted to administer the medication. Parents can give the marijuana dose(s) before and after school or during the day, but not on school grounds.

4112.85-R—All administrative regulations will be submitted by the school superintendent to the school board for review and approval prior to their implementation.

PERFORMANCE APPRAISAL FOR CLASSIFIED EMPLOYEES—REALLY?

The following is an example of a policy for the performance appraisal for classified employees. The example centers on five policy characteristics:

1. purposes of performance evaluations;
2. for whom the policy is directed;
3. when performance evaluations are to be administered;
4. performance evaluation and its relationship to pay increases; and
5. what evaluations do not do.

> Performance Appraisal—Classified Personnel　　　　　　　　Code GDO
> Assessment of employee performance, motivation for individual improvement, and realistic planning for future career development are three of the major objectives of the Board of Education. Based on these objectives, the Board believes a continuous program of performance appraisal is necessary for the purposes of recognizing and reinforcing appropriate performance job responsibilities, identifying and motivating improvement of standard performance, and fostering an atmosphere of high morale, cooperation, and productivity. The Classified Staff Performance Appraisal System is designed to be a yearlong active process involving both supervisor and employee participation.

The *preliminary* appraisal conference occurs no later than October 30. For employees hired after October 30, the preliminary appraisal conference should occur no later than forty-five days from the date of hire. Employees will not receive an employee rating during the preliminary conference. The *final appraisal conference* occurs in May, at which time employees will receive a performance rating. Completed appraisals are due to Human Resources by May 15. Performance ratings determine the annual pay increases, which are due July 1 for twelve-month employees. For less than twelve-month employees, pay increases are effective with the beginning of the school year assignment and are reflected in the September paycheck.

The performance appraisal does not create any contract of employment. Any failure of the district to follow the appraisal procedure does not limit the district's discretion to discipline, suspend, terminate, or any other job action that the district, in its discretion, considers necessary.

Source: Thompson School District R2-J, Loveland, Colorado. Produced by the Human Resources Department, December 2006.

A PRACTICE POLICY EXERCISE

The following proposed policy on academic freedom is given to you as school superintendent by the committee on teacher evaluation and professional development. If you approve the statement as written, you will take it to the school board for its examination and first reading. Your immediate task is to examine the policy proposal and determine if it is ready to be presented to the board. If not, what changes will you recommend? Can the policy statement be improved? If so, what must be done to improve it?

Wymore School District
School Personnel—Academic Freedom   Code: JB
The Wymore School District supports the teachers' freedom to think and express, to select appropriate instructional resources and adjust teaching methods to meet the learning style of each student. Such freedom carries with it the responsibility of using personal judgment and wise language that fosters student learning. Vulgar language will not be tolerated. The school district's student handbook asks students to report such use to the school principle.

Controversial issues may be discussed in the classroom if the teacher exercises the basic ethical responsibilities of the teaching profession such as the student maturity level. The use of professional ethics and good judgment in the selection of required readings and employment of materials and methods of learning is to be considered as fits the case. In each and every case, the teacher is required to: (1) be alert to any aspects of her lesson plan that could be discriminatory or harassment; (2) check with the appropriate person in the school before any discriminatory material is used; and (3) keep lesson plans used in the classroom after their use for evidence if charges are brought forth.

As previously stated, what must be done to improve the "policy" statement? As school superintendent, you can recommend specific changes in the policy, take action with the school board to adopt the policy as written, or reject the policy altogether. At this time, take a few minutes to identify minimum changes/corrections that you would recommend for the foregoing policy. Then, check your suggestions with those needed changes set forth as follows:

1. First of all, the policy code is incorrect. The code JB as listed refers to section J, Students, and subsection B, Academic Freedom. The policy centers on section G, Personnel, subsection B, Professional Personnel, and an added division, V, Academic Freedom. Thus, the code should read GBV.
2. In the first paragraph of the policy, the word principle must be corrected to principal.
3. The second line in paragraph one is unclear. The wording is more of a regulation than a policy that sets forth purposes and aims. Negative wording should be avoided (e.g., Vulgar language will not be tolerated). The revised wording is as follows: Freedom of speech carries with it the responsibility of using appropriate language that fosters effective communication. Such freedom carries with it the responsibility of using judgment and prudence to the end that it promotes effective communication and extends student understanding.
4. The third sentence in paragraph one is meaningless as stated. Wording must be changed to reflect an aim or purpose of effective language and a clear definition of the concept of "freedom of speech" for certificated personnel.
5. Paragraph two is faulty for several reasons. First and foremost, the paragraph is more of a regulation than a policy, especially in its discussion of requirements. The paragraph attempts to speak more to the matter of "how to do" rather than "what to do."

POLICY AND REGULATION AWARENESS: WITHOUT WHICH NOT

Policies that are not understood and followed by administrators, teachers, classified personnel, and students are useless. We have spoken previously about the fact that school policy manuals all too often just sit on the shelves of teachers' classrooms gathering dust. What strategies are needed to keep certificated and professional personnel and certified administrators aware of the policies and regulations that govern the school district?

Keeping school employees, students, and parents aware of school policies and regulations is the "without which not" of effective policy implementation.

How can students be kept aware of the school district's policies and regulations that directly impact on the conditions of their student rights and responsibilities? A statement of awareness of policies and administrative regulations is one effective strategy for answering these questions. We submit that employee/student/parent awareness is the key to effective policy and regulation effectiveness. For that reason, the following chapter sections present comprehensive examples of awareness documents/strategies for policy/regulation implementation.

Elementary students and secondary students in the Mesa district are given information and a guidance statement that each student must sign and verify that their teacher has talked to them about the school and classroom rules; that the student agrees to take home the statement and give it to his or her parents or guardian; and the fact that he or she understands that failure to follow the rules statement will result in disciplinary action. Figure 3.2 is a comprehensive example of a certificated administrator awareness statement as implemented by the Mesa Unified School District in Arizona. Similar awareness statements are used for certificated and classified employees. A comprehensive addendum also is included.

The following statement is presented as an example of one school district's awareness efforts and not one that is expected to meet the requirements of all such local school district statements in the state or the nation. In some instances, the following awareness statement appears to be "overcontrolling" even at the local school board level. Nevertheless, school employees are required to follow school board requirements. We would make a plea for more autonomy for classroom teachers to determine instruction that best meets the interests and needs of their students. An additional discussion of teacher autonomy is set forth later in the chapter.

In any case, the awareness statement below sets forth considerations of most importance relative to policy and regulation requirements with which school administrators/specialists must contend.

Figure 3.2: Administrator Statement of Awareness of Policies, Procedures, and Regulations—An Abstract
    Statement of Awareness of Policies, Procedures, and Regulations
                Certificated Administrators
Administrators are responsible for reviewing and complying with all policies, procedures, regulations, and other documents that govern their conduct, performance, and conditions of employment with the district. Administrators must provide employees with access to such documents.
    Employee Name:_____
    Employee Identification Number (EIN):_____
    School/Unit_____

Policy and Regulation Development

As an employee of the school district, I understand that the documents listed below are available to me for my review. I acknowledge and agree that I am responsible for reviewing and complying with all policies, procedures, regulations, and other documents that govern my conduct, performance, and conditions of employment as an employee of the district.

1. School District's Mission Statement
2. School District's Policies and Regulations Manual
3. Child Abuse Reporting Protocol
4. Employee Handbook
5. Information and Guidelines for Student Behavior
6. Student Handbook
7. Directives for Testing
8. Teacher or Staff Handbook
9. Evaluation Systems
10. Special Education Implementation Guidelines
11. Working Conditions and Benefits for Administrators
12. Working Conditions and Benefits for Classified Employees
13. Working Conditions and Benefits for Administrators
14. Working Conditions and Benefits for Classified Employees
15. Site Pay-for-Performance Goals/Incentive Program Guidelines
16. Curriculum and State Academic Standards
17. Emergency Response Plan
18. Hiring Practices for Certificated and Classified Personnel

Employee Signature:_____
Date:_____

(The Statement of Awareness for an Administrator will be signed and returned to Human Resources prior to the last day of August or within thirty days after the hire date for a new employee. The form will be kept in the employee's personnel file in the District office.)

ADDENDUM TO STATEMENT OF AWARENESS
ADMINISTRATOR/SPECIALIST

Many of the policies and procedures that give directions and govern the conditions and expectations of our employment are based on state and/or federal laws. It is your professional responsibility to be aware of applicable laws, statutes, and policies. The following laws and policies are specifically called to your attention. Policies and regulations are available on the District's Internet website as well.

ARS 13-3620—Reporting Child Abuse
All employees who, when acting in the scope of their employment, develop a reasonable belief that a minor has been or is the victim of child abuse (i.e., non-accidental injury, sexual abuse, or neglect) must *immediately* call law enforcement or the Department of Child Safety. In addition, a record of the call must be created using the On-Base system. For additional information, see Governing Board Policy JHG and the District's Child Abuse Reporting Protocol.

GBCA—Staff Conflict of Interest
Any employee who has an actual or potential conflict of interest in performing job duties for the District is obligated to disclose the conflict in writing in a timely fashion by delivering a Notice of Conflict of Interest memorandum to the employee's supervisor and to the Purchasing Department. An employee will not exercise direct control over another employee who is a family member, and employees who are family members will not work in the same school or department unless the superintendent approves an exception because the risk presented by a conflict is not significant or cannot be avoided without causing substantial harm to the District's operations. An employee must not participate in a District decision or vote where the employee or the employee's family member has, directly or indirectly, a substantial (i.e., monetary or ownership) interest in the purchase or sale of goods or services by the District, or in any other decision of the District. An employee will not enter into a contract for the sale of goods or services to the District unless the contract is awarded through public competitive bidding. The prohibition does not apply to contract for the sale of goods or services by an employee's spouse or other family member. Employees must not accept or solicit, directly or indirectly, any gifts, gratuity, favor, entertainment, or loan that is, or may appear to be, designed to influence the employee's official conduct. Employees may accept unsolicited advertising or promotional material of nominal value and food or refreshments that are incidental to a business meeting.

CBCX—Workplace Harassment-Employees
Workplace harassment of or by employees is prohibited. Workplace harassment includes sexual harassment or any other unwelcome verbal, written, or physical conduct that denigrates or shows hostility or aversion toward an individual on the basis of race, color, national origin, sex (including gender identity, sexual orientation, marital status, or pregnancy), disability, or age. *Any* employee who believes he or she has been sexually harassed should lodge a complaint with an appropriate supervisor or the Assistant Superintendent of Human Resources.

GBE—Staff-Safety and Health
Employees are to comply with safety and health standards, rules, and regulations, and chemical safety training requirements. An employee may be required to take a physical examination test if there is a reasonable belief that the employee lacks the strength, stamina, or other physical skill required by District policy or state law to perform the essential functions of the position held by the employee. The employee will receive forty-eight hours' notice prior to the test. An employee who refuses to attempt a physical performance test is subject to disciplinary action, including termination of employment.

GBH—Staff-Student Relations
The Governing Board expects employees to relate to students in a manner that maintains social and moral patterns of behavior consistent with acceptable professional conduct. When exercising general supervision over the conduct of students, employees will treat students with dignity and respect. Code GHBR

describes specific expectations concerning professional boundaries between employees and students. Each employee is responsible for reading and complying with this regulation.

GBKB—Drugs and Alcohol

The District facilitates a safe environment for students, employees, and the community by requiring a drug-free workplace mandated by state and federal laws. Any employee arrested, cited, or charged with a drug- and/or alcohol-related criminal offense (e.g., DUI), whether a felony or a misdemeanor, must notify his or her immediate supervisor no later than forty-eight hours after such event. The term "charge" includes a charge, indictment, information, or complaint. Any conviction for a drug- and/or alcohol-related offense must be reported to the District, in writing, no later than five days after the conviction. Any employee arrested, cited, charged with, or convicted of any such offense who fails to notify his or her immediate supervisor will be subject to disciplinary action, including termination.

GSBA—Employee Technology Use

Employees are to use District technology for school-related purposes and the performance of job duties. District technology includes computers, telephones, cell phones, and radio communications equipment, telecommunications networks, and Internet access that are owned, leased, or controlled by the District. Incidental, occasional personal use of District computers is permitted as long as it does not result in any additional cost to the District and does not interfere with the employee's job duties and performance, with the system operations, or with other system users. Any employee who violates this policy or the rules governing use of District computers is subject to disciplinary action, up to and including discharge. Illegal uses of District computers will also result in referral to law enforcement authorities.

GCPD—Disciplinary Action—Professional Staff & GDPD-Support Staff: Disciplinary Action of Misconduct: Dismissal for Unsatisfactory Performance

These policies define misconduct, list types of misconduct, outline methods of disciplinary action that can be taken, and explain the process for suspension and/or dismissal of an employee for unsatisfactory performance or misconduct. Misconduct includes:

- Failing to report to his or her supervisor within forty-eight hours of any arrest, charge, citation, indictment, information complaint, conviction, or plea agreement involving (a) a felony, regardless of its nature or seriousness; or (b) a misdemeanor involving drugs or alcohol (including, without limitation, driving while impaired) or moral turpitude (including, without limitation, indecent exposure and any offense that may require an offender to register as a sex offender).
- Violating the protocol or established norms for administration of a test or assessment, or falsifying or misrepresenting data from the administration of a test or assessment.

GDK—Support Staff Workday
All classified personnel, other than supervisors and administrators, must record all hours worked and are subject to time reporting guidelines as specified in GDK-R.

IF/IFE/IGA—Curriculum, Academic Standards, and Instruction
The State Board of Education requires the Governing Board, superintendent, and each school principal to sign a Declaration of Curriculum and Instructional Alignment to the Arizona Academic Standards. Policies IF, IFE, IGA require certificated teachers to familiarize themselves with the District and state standards and to integrate the District and state standards into their teaching area, to participate in training related to their District and state standards, and to integrate the District and state standards into their instructional practices to the extent that such standards apply to their teaching area. Certificated teachers will be evaluated to assess whether they integrate District and state standards into their instructional practices to the extent that such standards apply to their teaching area.

IIBE—Video Use
A video may be viewed by students during a school course, class, or extracurricular activity or a school-sponsored activity if the content and use are appropriate and the use will not violate the rights of the copyright owner. For any video not rated G or equivalent, a Video Use Request form must be completed and signed by the school principal or designee, and the parent of any student who is under age eighteen must give written permission for the student to view the video.

JB—Equal Educational Opportunities
The District maintains a safe and supporting learning environment and will ensure that students are not excluded from participation in, denied benefits of, or otherwise subjected to discrimination in any program or activity on the basis of race, color, national origin, religion, sex, or disability.

JFD—Student Harassment and Bullying
Harassment and bullying are prohibited on campus, in school vehicles, at school bus stops, while students are traveling to and from school, and during school-sponsored events. An employee with knowledge of harassment or bullying behavior against a student must report that behavior to the school principal, employee's supervisor, or to any administrator or supervisor to whom the employee feels comfortable making the report. Students and staff involved in harassment or bullying of students will be subject to disciplinary consequences.

Harassment means abusive conduct that is directed at one or more students because of the student's actual or perceived race, color, national origin, religion, sex (including gender, identity, sexual orientation, marital status, or pregnancy), or disability and that is sufficiently severe, pervasive, or persistent so as to interfere with or limit the student's ability to participate or benefit from the services, activities, or opportunities offered by the school. It includes sexual harassment.

Bullying means any aggressive, intentional behavior carried out by a person or group repeatedly and over time against a victim who cannot easily defend himself or herself. Bullying requires an observed or perceive imbalance of power—such as physical strength, access to embarrassing information, or popularity—between the bully and victim. Bullying may be verbal, physical, or relational. It includes cyberbullying and retaliation for reporting complaint of harassment or bullying.

JGA—Student Behavior Management and Intervention
Teachers and other instructional staff assigned to work with students with behavior problems are authorized to use seclusion or a restraint to respond to a student who creates an immediate risk of harm to himself or herself, other students, or staff. The student will be released from seclusion or a restraint as soon as the student regains self-control. The school principal will make reasonable attempts to notify the student's parents by the end of the same day that seclusion restraint is used. A written note must also be sent home and the incident recorded in the student's education records.

JGB—Alternatives to Student Suspension
Teachers may detain students after school to make up work for disciplinary reasons. Parents/guardians must be notified if students are to be retained after school for more than fifteen minutes or will miss a bus. School principals may assign a student to an alternative learning classroom or alternative school in lieu of out-of-school suspension.

JN—Student Fees and Charges
Principals are authorized to waive or reduce student fees for hardship. Students in elementary schools will be charged reasonable fees for optional extracurricular activities. Students in secondary schools will be charged reasonable fees for extracurricular activities, on-campus parking, and fine arts and career and technical education courses.

JO—Student Records
Student educational records are confidential and must not be divulged without parental consent as specifically authorized by policy.

KBAA—Parental Involvement
The state of Arizona requires that parents have an opportunity to review a list of parent rights and responsibilities concerning a range of issues. The list is provided in this policy/regulation.

AN ADDED STRATEGY FOR STUDENT AWARENESS

School districts nationally have implemented information and guideline statements for elementary and secondary students. Such awareness statements commonly include student information relative to student responsibilities, general student information, guidelines for student behavior, student due process rights, problem areas, search and seizure, and bus rules. For example, within the topic of problem areas, such student responsibilities and consequences as academic misconduct/cheating, alcohol violation, bus violation, dangerous weapon/instrument, defiance of authority/disrespect, drug violation, fighting, harassment/bullying, student speech, theft, tardiness, absenteeism, use of cellphones, truancy/unexcused absence, and vandalism commonly are included.

In addition, a statement of student awareness form is abbreviated and must be signed by the student as having been received and understood by the student. The student must verify the fact that the student's parents have been provided access to the awareness document.

CHAPTER SNAPSHOT

School District Policy and Its Importance in Serious Student Hearings

The opportunity to observe a student hearing relative to expulsion underscores the importance of school district policies and regulations. A due process hearing is most often required in serious cases of student expulsion. As pointed out by Peterson, Rossmiller, and Volz (1978), "The professional staff may not expel pupils unless specifically authorized by statute" (p. 352). Therefore, it is of paramount importance that school administrators be well informed of state statutes and implement expulsion procedures to the letter.

The purpose here is to point out the relevance of policy and regulations in the procedures that must be followed in student hearings—in this case, student expulsion. The details of the case observed are not reported here; rather, the frequency of policy references within the hearing procedure is the focus of this snapshot. At the very outset of the student hearing, the behavioral record of the student was set forth; specifically, policy codes JIC and JK and regulation JK-R, student discipline, student conduct, and the regulation relating to student discipline were stated as the primary reasons for the recommendation of expulsion.

Later in the hearing, the state statutes concerning the specific serious charges against the student were identified. The state's expulsion policies regarding open defiance, absenteeism, and age for expulsion were presented. Each of the student violations related to the state statutes and was verified one by one. The matter of student and parent awareness of the school policies and regulations was discussed in depth. Policy and regulation awareness activities were reviewed; the student awareness handbook and the request for parental verification of receiving and reading the student policies/regulations were presented by the school principal. The school principal described the sessions held with students in regard to the student handbook that set forth student behavior requirements.

Specific sections of the student handbook that related to student discipline, disruption of the education program, endangerment of student safety, and school property were presented, among the student's violations, and verified with examples by the school principal. Other violations of such matters as unexcused absences and serious "injury" problems were noted and clarified by references to school district policies. Matters pertinent to the case at hand including closed campus, stealing, possession of firearms, as presented in the policies and student handbook, were reported. One exhibit, policy code JIC, was presented relative to student conduct.

Speech that is not expected on the part of students, the responsibility for knowing school rules, and other violations of city laws and other related mandates were prominent in the hearing. Policies/regulations related to excessive absenteeism, expulsion, off-campus violations, stealing, and the school board policy on expulsion were noted as being warranted in the instances of violations presented by the school principal.

Once again, the question of notifying students relative to the school's conduct codes was brought up for clarification. The principal referred to the student handbook, the school's awareness activities, and the required awareness responses to be signed by students, parents, and teachers. The disruption of the school's program and student learning was examined in relation to the student's reported violations. Once again, the policies, regulations, and state laws relating to these matters were reported. Relevant policies, regulations, and state statutes dominated the presentation of evidence in this student hearing.

SNAPSHOT SUMMARY

The purpose of presenting the primary procedures of the foregoing student hearing was to underscore the paramount importance of school leaders having a high level of knowledge and skills related to governance policy, its content, and its use. It seems clear that school leaders who do not operate with a basic knowledge of the policies under which the school must operate will not be successful.

Notification of Student Due Process Rights

The Mesa School District's *Information & Guidelines Student Handbook for Secondary Students* (2016–2017) includes the due process rights of all students. The definition of expulsion, procedures relative to student expulsion, and hearing appeal procedures are set forth in the following section.

Expulsion
Expulsion means the permanent withdrawal of the privilege of attending any school in the district, unless the Governing Board reinstates that privilege. Only the Governing Board can expel a student. Expulsion takes place only after a formal hearing is conducted and the Governing Board has made a decision to expel. If the assistant superintendent believes that expulsion is appropriate, the assistant gives written notice to the student and parent that expulsion is being recommended and that a hearing will take place. The student and parent are given notice of applicable due process procedure.

The parent and student subject to expulsion are given notice of the date, time, and place of the hearing at least five working days prior to the hearing.

All expulsion hearings are conducted by an independent hearing officer who hears the evidence, prepares a report, and brings a recommendation to the board for action. The hearing is closed to protect the privacy of the student unless the parents request that it be open to the public.

The hearing officer's recommendation may be appealed by sending written notice of appeal to the board within five working days after receipt of the hearing officer's recommendation. The notice of appeal must be received no less than twenty-four hours prior to the board meeting or session where the hearing officer's recommendation and any appeal are considered. The board is the ultimate authority in the district and is not bound to accept the hearing officer's recommendation.

EXTERNAL INFLUENCES ON PUBLIC SCHOOL PROGRAMS: HEAVY HANG OVER THY HEAD

Unfortunate conflicts as revealed in the snapshot generally are more complicated than one might think. In fact, various court cases have ruled on such matters as teacher placement and teacher assigned duties. Court cases, state statutes, teacher contracts, and school board policies/regulations commonly control problems as revealed in the foregoing snapshot. One might contend that, for example, filling in for another teacher is a common practice in their school situation. However, as the saying goes, it isn't a problem until it's a problem.

If, indeed, the school district's policy had stated that teachers would be responsible for fulfilling other teaching duties/assignments as determined by the school principal or the teacher's contract stated an assignment of teaching vocal music and other teaching assignments in the best interests of the school's program and its students, the problem most likely would have been resolved. Refusal to comply would be considered insubordination on the part of the teacher, and discipline, including suspension and/or dismissal, would be a possible outcome.

The teacher's contract looms important in such cases. For example, if a teacher's contract states that the teacher is to teach grade 3 in the elementary school, he or she cannot be assigned to another grade without the teacher's approval. Similarly, if the teacher's contract states that he or she is to teach science courses, the teacher cannot be assigned to teach social studies without his or her approval (Peterson, Rossmiller, & Volz, 1978). Among other things, the foregoing snapshot serves to underscore the vital importance of school board policies on numerous matters, many of which were reported in previous sections of the chapter.

As mentioned in chapter 1, the federal laws, court rulings, and state statutes have great influence on the policies and regulations of local school districts. The Urbana, Illinois, School District, for example, listed 281 specific policy topics that were based on statutes of the state legislature. As noted by the Center for Public Education (2006), "Each day, districts are beholden to a staggering list of laws, regulations, rules, and policies that motivate and control behavior. Federal, state, and local governments generate reams of expectations. Court decisions are unending. Requirements are highly complicated and ultimately determine what board members, employees, and students must do or are forbidden to do" (p. 1).

THE UNITED STATES CONSTITUTION AND ITS GUARANTEE OF RIGHTS, PRIVILEGES, AND PROTECTIONS

If one were to trace the lifeline of many school policies and regulations, the line ultimately would end with the establishment of the U.S. Constitution. As noted by the Center for Public Education (2006), "In the last 30 years, schools have evolved into a battleground for legal and policy skirmishes on the most contentious moral and cultural issues in American life. School districts serve as a kind of mirror, reflecting society's hopes, dreams, and fears" (p. 2).

The foregoing contention is revealed in the requirements set forth in various amendments of the Constitution as illustrated below:

The First Amendment prohibits the making of any law respecting an establishment of religion, ensuring that there is no prohibition on free exercise of religion, abridging the freedom of speech, infringing on the freedom of the press, interfering with the right to peaceable assemble, or prohibiting the petitioning for a government redress of grievances (adopted December 15, 1791).

The Fourth Amendment to the U.S. Constitution prohibits unreasonable searches and seizures and requires any warrant to be judicially sanctioned and supported by probable cause (adopted 1791).

The Fifth Amendment creates a number of rights relevant to both criminal and civil legal proceedings. In criminal cases, the Fifth Amendment guarantees the right to a grand jury, forbids "double jeopardy," and protects against self-incrimination. It also requires that "due process of law" be part of any proceeding that denies a citizen "life, liberty, or property" and requires the government to compensate citizens when it takes private property for public use (adopted September 25, 1789).

The Fourteenth Amendment addresses citizenship rights and equal protection of the law and was proposed in response to issues related to former slaves following the Civil War. The due process clause prohibits state and local government from depriving persons of life, liberty, and pursuit of happiness without legislative authorization (approved July 9, 1868).

Authorities point out that the school board has two sides of the legal equation when it comes to public school education: compliance and prevention (Darden, 2006, April 5). *Compliance* centers on the duty for the school board to obey the law. School boards are expected to stay abreast of the law and to take the necessary steps to be in compliance with it. In addition, Darden notes, "Besides worrying about the Constitution, school districts also must fret about federal statutes, legal initiatives, and statewide legislation. Compliance is a never-ending and meticulous task" (p. 2).

Prevention is the actions that need to be taken to avoid legal problems, including lawsuits. The key to compliance is vested in the action that a school board takes to maintain an updated and accurate policy system that directs the school district on an effective but legal path.

KEY CHAPTER IDEAS AND RECOMMENDATIONS

- The school district board of education's primary responsibility is the development of policy that serves to direct and guide the direction of the school district. School board members, therefore, must be knowledgeable of the importance and need of policy development. Local control of education demands such attention.
- School boards adopt policy, and the school superintendent and staff take appropriate steps to develop related regulations that implement the adopted policies.
- Local control of education has its pros and cons. The chapter information supports the concept that the local school district personnel are in the best position to determine the educational program that best meets the interests and needs of the school district's students. Although state legislatures, federal laws, and court decisions greatly influence the policy provisions for local schools, local school personnel must be directly involved in

the development of policies and regulations that control the educational program.
- Effective policy resolves most conflicts before they become serious problems. Therefore, awareness is the "without which not" of effective policy/regulation development and implementation.
- Awareness of policies and regulations depends greatly on a planned program led by the superintendent of schools. Awareness of policy must focus on students, teachers, classified personnel, administrators, parents, and school community members.
- The legal requirements established by the Constitution of the United States, the state legislatures, state educational departments, the courts, federal law, and the local school board have great influence on school policies. The hands of school personnel tend to be tied for becoming directly involved in the politics that determine school matters. One school superintendent sent a letter to the parents of students encouraging them to contact their congressional representative to vote against a certain pending statute that was not best for school needs. The superintendent was highly criticized for meddling in such political matters. Yet,

> Public education is a political activity; as such, it is a fertile arena for conflict. Conflict provides opportunity to examine, clarify, and compare the mission (purposes and function) of the school with the wants and needs of the society it serves. . . . We no longer can accept the myth that education is apolitical. Politics, not baseball, is America's favorite pastime, and for the American educational system it is serious business. (Norton, Webb, Dlugosh, & Sybouts, 1978, pp. 87, 101)

- Awareness of policies and regulations on the part of school personnel and the school community in general is essential. Awareness must be monitored and controlled under the leadership of the school superintendent.

DISCUSSION QUESTIONS

1. Chapter 3 emphasized the importance of policy and regulation development in relation to local control. What is meant by local control in this statement, and how is local control revealed best in school district policy development?
2. Discuss the matter of policy and regulation development from the standpoint of having them "derived" primarily at the local school district level or using the state's school board association to develop the school district's policies.

3. Chapter 3 contends that effective school district policies serve to resolve conflicts before they become serious problems. Give several examples of how this contention is valid.
4. As school superintendent, you are asked how the school district's policies and regulations are kept "alive and working." How might you respond?
5. Consider the importance of school district and employee employment contracts and job descriptions relative to the legal consideration that these statements hold for administrative operations in the school district. For example, why is teacher placement an important consideration in relation to a teaching position in the school district?

CASE STUDIES

Case Study 1—That's Not in My Contract!

Edward Bannister had served as a music teacher at Wymore High School for twenty-seven years. One morning before his first class, Ed was in the music room planning his Friday night's performance for students and parents. Elsie Rosen, school principal, was faced with an emergency and was seeking teachers to fill in for the industrial arts teacher who was ill and would be absent for the day.

Elsie approached Ed in the classroom, explained the situation to him, and asked for his help in filling in for the industrial arts teacher during third period, Ed's planning period. The music teacher explained that he was using the planning period to do more work on the Friday night music program. "I'd like to help, but I need that time to prepare my music program," pleaded Ed.

"But, we've got to cover the absence somehow, and I have tried all other avenues," said Principal Rosen. "You just have to help me out on this one."

"Just a minute," responded Ed. "I can't oblige you and I really do not have to. My teaching contract says that I was employed to teach music, and that's what I plan to do. I can't be forced to do something or even appear in a class that isn't part of the contract that I signed."

Principal Rosen hurried out of the room and headed for the telephone to call the director of human resources.

Discussion Questions

1. Was Ed Bannister, the teacher, right in the stand that he took in this matter? Or is he likely to be charged with insubordination?
2. Assume that you are the school superintendent in this case, and Principal Rosen reports the happenings of this situation to you on the phone. How would you reply and/or act to resolve this matter?
3. What might have resolved this matter in the first place?

Case Study 2—But I Am on My Break and I Have Business to Attend to

Rosanna Gomez was in the school office to use the computer to send an email message to a secondary school journal editor regarding the progress of his manuscript on his student project of using instruments brought to school by his students to teach a unit on fractions. The school district policy for use of school computers, long-distance telephone calls, and other school devices stated, "Employees are to use District technology for school-related purposes and the performance of job duties. District technology includes computers, telephones, cell phones, radio communications networks, and Internet access that is owned, leased, or controlled by the District. Use of such equipment for personal business purposes in prohibited. In special cases, use of such property must receive the permission of the school principal."

Principal Emory Washington walked into the office and saw Rosanna at the computer. With the email message sent, Rosanna greeted the principal as she walked out of the office. Immediately, the school secretary, Alberta Woolhether, informed principal Washington that Miss Gomez had sent an email to a journal editor in New York. She also reported that she had informed Miss Gomez that permission to use the computer might be in order. Secretary Woolhether also reported that Miss Gomez had said that such a rule was out of order for professional personnel.

Case Study Discussion

Assume the role of Principal Washington and think about what you should do in this case. The district regulation on the use of District technology is quite clear: it is to be used only for school purposes. Is additional information about this matter in order, or do you have enough information to act accordingly? Be specific in your response. That is, do not merely state that you need to find out more about the nature of the emails. If this is the case, what specific questions and/or evidence do you plan to collect?

REFERENCES

Chisholm, L. L. (1953). *The work of the modern high school.* New York: Macmillan.
Center for Public Education. (2006). Alexandria, VA: National School Boards Association.
Darden, E. C. (2006, April 5). *The law and its influence on public school districts: An overview.*
Employment Policy Foundation. (2003, August 15). *Phased retirement: Its time has come.* In partnership with the Sloan Foundation, Washington, DC.

Lamiell, P. (2012, February 10). *How should politics influence education policy.* New York: Columbia University, Teachers College Newsroom.

National Center for Educational Statistics (2013–2014). U.S. Department of Education's Institute of Educational Services. Washington, DC.

Norton, M. S. (2008). *Executive leadership for effective administration.* Boston: Allyn & Bacon-Pearson.

Norton, M. S., Webb, L. D., Dlugosh, L. L., & Sybouts, W. (1996). *The school superintendency: New responsibilities, new leadership.* Needham Heights, MA: Allyn & Bacon.

Parkinson, C. (1978). *Towards a philosophy of administration.* Oxford: Basil Blackwell.

Peterson, L. J., Rossmiller, R. A., & Volz, M. M. (1978). *The law and public school operation.* New York: Harper & Row.

Thompson School District (2006). *Performance appraisal: Classified.* Human Resources Department, Loveland, CO: Author.

Chapter 4

Impact of Federal Laws, State Statutes, and the Courts on Local School District Policy

Primary Chapter Goal: To underscore the influence of federal involvement, state statutes, and court rulings on local school district policy making; the pros and cons of such controls; the school board issues and the models that demonstrate effective policy implementation; and recommendations for improving school board member qualifications.

THE RELATIONSHIPS OF POLICIES, REGULATIONS, AND BYLAWS TO STATE AND NATIONAL LAWS

State and national laws supersede school board policies, regulations, and bylaws. A *law* is a rule recognized by the nation or state as binding on its members (Norton, 2008). Laws that emanate from governing bodies such as state legislatures and the United States Congress or court rulings commonly are stated verbatim in the policy manuals of school districts. For example, procedures for dismissing a tenured teacher or student expulsion increasingly are included in the school district's policy manual word for word.

In such cases as teacher dismissal and student expulsion, school districts have lost hearings and court decisions because the procedures followed by the school district were not in compliance with the state statute. It is quite clear that federal and state legislative acts and court decisions on matters of education are directing the development of policy making in school districts at an ever-increasing rate. Developing effective school policies at the local school level is a difficult and time-consuming task. Nevertheless, relevant policy decision making is the most important job of positive school board operations. A note to board members: That's why you were elected!

THE INFLUENCE OF FEDERAL MANDATES ON STATE AND LOCAL POLICY DEVELOPMENT

If one were to trace the lifeline of many school policies and regulations, the line ultimately would end with the establishment of the U.S. Constitution. As noted by the Center for Public Education (2006), "In the last 30 years, schools have evolved into a battleground for legal and policy skirmishes on the most contentious moral and cultural issues in American life. School districts serve as a kind of mirror, reflecting society's hopes, dreams, and fears" (p. 2). The foregoing contention is revealed in the requirements set forth in various amendments of the Constitution as illustrated below:

The First Amendment prohibits the making of any law respecting an establishment of religion, ensuring that there is no prohibition on free exercise of religion; abridging the freedom of speech; infringing on the freedom of the press; interfering with the right to peaceable assemble; or petitioning for a government redress of grievances (adopted December 15, 1791).

The Fourth Amendment to the U.S. Constitution prohibits unreasonable searches and seizures and requires any warrant to be judicially sanctioned and supported by probate cause (adopted 1791).

The Fifth Amendment creates a number of rights relevant to both criminal and civil legal proceedings. In criminal cases, the Fifth Amendment guarantees the right to a grand jury, forbids "double jeopardy," and protects against self-incrimination. It also requires that "due process of law" be part of any proceeding that denies a citizen "life, liberty, or property" and requires the government to compensate citizens when it takes private property for public use (adopted September 25, 1789).

The Fourteenth Amendment addresses citizenship rights and equal protection of the law, and was proposed in response to issues related to former slaves following the Civil War. The due process clause prohibits state and local government from depriving persons of life, liberty, and pursuit of happiness without legislative authorization (approved July 9, 1868).

Authorities point out that the school board has two sides of the legal equation when it comes to public school education, compliance and prevention (Center for Public Education, 2006, April 5). *Compliance* centers on the duty for the school board to obey the law. School boards are expected to stay abreast of the law and to take the necessary steps to be in compliance with it. *Prevention* involves the actions that need to be taken to avoid legal problems, including lawsuits. The key to compliance is vested in the action that a school board takes to maintain an updated and accurate policy system that directs the school district in an effective but legal path.

Best estimates indicate that current public elementary and secondary school financial support is federal, 18.0 percent; state, 45.2 percent; and local, 36.8 percent. Statistical reports tend to differ widely. For example, state per-pupil support for education ranges from $6,546 in Utah to $20,577 in Washington, DC. The per-pupil state annual support exceeded $15,000 in eight states (National Center for Educational Statistics, 2013–2014).

ATTEMPTS TO PASS LOCAL CONTROL OF EDUCATION LEGISLATION AT THE CONGRESSIONAL LEVEL

On January 7, 2015, Senator David Vitter of Louisiana introduced the Local Control of Education Act that was designed to prohibit the federal government from directly or indirectly mandating, incentivizing, or coercing states to adopt the common core standard or any other specific standards, instructional content, curricula, assessments, or programs of instruction. The bill did not track beyond the introductory stage. Recent political maneuvers have contended that the national attempts to implement common core programs would recede, but they have not at the time of this writing.

The department of education in most states has set forth advice on the policies and documents that governing bodies and proprietors of schools are required by law to have. For example, one section of statutory policies required by education legislation in one state included capability of staff, school behavior, sex education, special education needs, teacher appraisal, and teachers' pay. Data protection and health and safety policies were required by other legislation.

Other statutory requirements have included freedom of information, admission arrangements, central record of recruitment and vetting checks, complaint procedure statement, equality information and objectives, register of pupil attendance, staff discipline, conduct, and grievance procedures. Documents referenced in statutory guidance have focused on child protection policy and procedures, procedures for dealing with allegations of abuse, and supporting pupils with medical conditions. We view policy adoption as an authority given by the state legislature to the school board alone. However, the foregoing information illustrates the major involvement of federal influences.

The increasing scope of state and federal involvement in educational actions has standardized such factors as instructional policy and standards that must be met. The school board's discretion regarding policy decisions has been reduced by increasing regulations from the state legislatures. Special interest groups, professional councils, and commissions have increased their influence on school academic standards and local decision making.

School districts are less able to control their own destiny. Indicating that school boards must assume more responsibility for implementing effective policy measures locally is, of course, a simplification of the situation at hand. Most everyone would agree that those persons who will be affected by governance policies tend to support what they help create, so those who will be affected by policies should have input to them (Arkansas School Boards Association, 2006, p. 5).

MOVES TOWARD THE RETURN OF LOCAL GOVERNANCE CONTROL

Recently, the State Board of Education of New Jersey (2016) moved closer to full local control over the area of personnel. Personnel is one of five functional areas of education; Governance, Fiscal Management, Operations, and Instruction complete the list. Because the Newark Public School District scored 100 percent in the area of personnel, and the school district had demonstrated "substantial and sustained" progress in that area, the district was given local control for personnel matters. In addition, Newark received an equivalency for the area of instruction and program, a pathway for the district to demonstrate evidence of substantial and sustained progress in that area.

New Jersey's school monitoring system sets forth the standards required for school districts to achieve substantial and sustained progress. The Newark school district scored 100 percent in the area of personnel and therefore was recommended for return to local control. The commissioner of education, David G. Hespe, was of the opinion that Newark was on pace to obtain full local control.

The action of the State Board of Education of New Jersey was revolutionary in many ways; such actions certainly are historic. Steps of progress by the local school board in other functional areas could well lead to full local control of education. The example set by the state of New Jersey demonstrates the leadership that should inspire school boards nationally to adopt similar programs.

THE PROS AND CONS REGARDING LOCAL CONTROL OF EDUCATION

Local control was discussed in chapter 2. Its importance to the policy governance activities of school boards is such that we take time to reemphasize the "arguments" for local control of education at the local level versus federal intervention and state mandates set forth for curriculum and student achievement standards. One might agree or disagree with the following pros and cons regarding local control of education. Nevertheless, we believe that it is only fair and important that readers know the common views on local versus external control of education policy.

The *pros* for local control of education include the following contentions:

1. The quality of teaching and learning effectiveness can be improved because the school is administered by the individuals and boards most knowledgeable about the school community and its students' interests and needs. As such, administrators, teachers, parents, and community members have a direct interest in the immediate and future success of students who are attending or have attended the local schools.
2. Because school purposes and policy decisions are determined by representative school board members, the governance process includes a close working relationship with members of the community. In turn, community support is fostered.
3. External control is eliminated or substantially reduced, which facilitates positive decision making and meaningful administrative regulations that can be readily implemented in programs for student learning.
4. Rather than increasing student achievement academically, external control of the school curriculum leads to an emphasis on mandated testing rather than on effective teaching. The lack of teacher autonomy becomes problematic and reportedly increases teacher turnover.
5. Local school governance evolves from the culture of the local school community. Policies should be developed on the basis of cultural sanctions and goals of the local school community. Externally developed policies do not meet this criterion.
6. Certain external control developments such as school district consolidation commonly result in increases in administrative bureaucracy, student personnel problems, and major emphasis on sports as opposed to academic achievement. Teachers with smaller classes are more able to know the interests and needs of their students than educators in larger school populations.

The *cons* of local control of education include the following contentions:

1. Some criticism of local control points to bureaucratic red tape that commonly surrounds contradictory views of what's best for education.
2. Local control has been in effect historically without evidence that student learning is being competitive with other nations. There has been a loss of confidence of local school control to provide high-quality education for all students. Certain major problems/issues have been overlooked by local politics, including civil rights, student rights, bilingual education, and

special education. In addition, local resistance to finance education is in evidence in a reluctance to pay property tax.
3. Low or undetermined student achievement standards set forth at the local level have resulted in failed test results. Academic standards are missing in most local school districts.
4. There are far too many local school districts with too many school boards to be able to develop and retain quality educational programs for all students in many curricular areas, including the area of special student needs.
5. Small, local school districts commonly are not able to attract and retain quality teacher and administrative personnel. In many situations, the school administrator is devoting his or her time to classroom teaching as opposed to matters of instruction and student learning.
6. Localizing control of education would inherently cause poorer communities and cities to fall behind in education. States with older residents who do not have children do not want to support education financially.
7. Local control means that there would be no standard levels of competency; everyone would have a different education. Such variance in education is contrary to the mobility of the nation's population. There is no assurance that a similar curriculum is being followed.

SCHOOL BOARDS AND LOCAL CONTROL OF EDUCATION

Unfortunate conflicts in the area of personnel relations are more complicated that one might think. In fact, various court cases have ruled on such matters as teacher placement and teacher assigned duties. Court cases, state statutes, teacher contracts, and school board policies/regulations commonly control personnel issues/problems. One might contend that such matters as having one teacher fill in for another who is absent is a common practice in a school situation. However, as the saying goes, it isn't a problem until it's a problem. Yet, court cases have ruled on similar personnel problems.

If the school district's policy stated that teachers would be responsible for fulfilling other teaching duties/assignments as determined by the school principal, or that the teacher's contract specified that the teacher would be teaching vocal music and other teaching assignments in the best interests of the school's program and its students, filling in for an absent teacher most likely would be an acceptable practice. Refusal to comply with such a request would be considered insubordination on the part of the teacher. Discipline, including suspension and/or dismissal, would be a possible outcome.

The teacher's contract is important in determining assignments. For example, if a teacher's contract states that he is to teach grade 3 in the elementary school, the teacher cannot be assigned to another grade without the teacher's approval.

Similarly, if the teacher's contract states that she is to teach science courses, the teacher cannot be assigned to teach social studies without her approval (Peterson, Rossmiller, & Volz, 1978). Among other things, the foregoing information serves to underscore the vital importance of school board policies on numerous matters, many of which were reported in previous sections of the chapter.

WHAT IS THE GOAL TO BE ACHIEVED?

As mentioned in chapter 1, the federal laws, court rulings, and state statutes have great influence on the policies and regulations of local school districts. The Urbana, Illinois, School District, for example, listed 281 specific policy topics that were based on statutes of the state legislature. As noted by the Center for Public Education (2006), "Each day, districts are beholden to a staggering list of laws, regulations, rules, and policies that motivate and control behavior. Federal, state, and local governments generate reams of expectations. Court decisions are unending. Requirements are highly complicated and ultimately determine what board members, employees, and students must do or are forbidden to do" (p. 1).

When we speak of local control, it is not to suggest that the entire responsibility for education in America be given to local school districts. Constitutionally, education is a state responsibility. We submit that the state's responsibility should be vested in broad, worthy purposes. However, the purposes should be stated as aims and ends to be achieved, rather than controls that inhibit local school district discretion or attempt to mandate how the desired ends are to be administered. The aims should encourage local creativity and flexibility that is needed for meeting individual student needs and interests. To accomplish this end, school board effectiveness in policy governance must be improved.

WHAT SCHOOL BOARDS MUST DO OR STOP DOING

One authority recommends that school boards focus their energies on effective policy making that establishes purposes and standards for program excellence rather than attempting to manage the district's business affairs (Bell, 1988). In addition, school boards must pay attention to the status of their policy system relative to its goals and procedures and the separate areas of policy making and educational administration. More attention needs to be paid to cooperative efforts among employee organizations and other state groups to initiate local school policy and recommend policy for the consideration of state agencies.

SCHOOL BOARD POLICY DEVELOPMENT: FOLLOWSHIP OR LEADERSHIP?

Just as the power structures of school boards differ, so do they differ in policy development.

> The key difference is the PG (policy governance) moves the board from a position of followship to one of leadership without becoming part of management (Ballantyne, 2006). With PG the board writes policy that says what the organization must accomplish . . . and through monitoring the board hold the staff accountable for achieving it. With traditional governance (TG) the board is more focused on oversight. It relies on demanding and evaluating a variety of management reports to ensure that the staff is behaving appropriately. When there is concern about how the staff is managing, TG boards often resort to edict-of-instruction. These edicts bring the board into the realm of management (Ballantyne, 2006).

THE POLICY GOVERNANCE MODEL

Policy governance, originally credited to John Carver, establishes three primary responsibilities of the school board: (1) Ownership Linkage—connecting with owners to learn their values about the ends that are desired and means that would be unacceptable; (2) Policy Development—writing those values as guidance for the board itself; and (3) Assurance of Organizational Performance—measuring to ensure that the organization demonstrates reasonable progress toward desired ends and reasonable compliance with policy guideline means (Wikipedia, 2016). In regard to education, ownership refers to the citizens of the school community.

Authorities underscore six points for governance emphasis for school boards that focus on an outward vision rather than an internal preoccupation:

1. Encouragement of diversity in viewpoints—owners of the school district, its citizens, are important persons in the process of determining values, beliefs, needs, and purposes that should guide educational pursuits for children and youth.
2. Strategic leadership more than administrative detail—the board defines and guides the appropriate relationships between the school district's "owners," the school board and the school superintendent. This does not infer a wide division of working relationships; policies and regulations are inextricably related, and positive communication between the school board and school staff are ongoing.

3. Clear distinction of board and school superintendent roles—the school board states what the school system is to achieve and provides the necessary discretion for the school superintendent to develop procedures for achieving the desired ends.
4. Collective rather than individual decisions—cooperative involvement in determining school purposes and means for achieving them. It always is wise for the school superintendent to review proposed administrative regulations with the school board. Such behavior gives evidence that the school superintendent and staff are doing their job and also provides an opportunity for both parties to determine whether they are on the same page regarding the policies at hand.
5. Future rather than past or present—emphasis on current programming is based on the school community's vision of the future program ends.
6. Productivity rather than reactivity—the school board develops policy and informs the school superintendent and his or her staff of what is to be done. Boards are developing policy rather than just reacting to policy matters.

The school board both articulates the ends to be achieved and monitors the extent to which the ends are being achieved.

CHAPTER SNAPSHOT

Roger Moe was a newly elected school board member. His father, Henri Moe, previously had served on the Fairview School District board for three terms. Roger was especially interested in doing a good job in his new role; his father had encouraged him to run for the school board position but set up the expectation that Roger was to do a good job if elected.

The school board had just initiated a new vocational/tech program that was to be housed on the property of a vacated air force base. The program would have more than sufficient space for its program offerings but needed special equipment for programs in auto mechanics, electronics, nursing aides, auto body shop, and others. Roger Moe was employed by an agricultural business that sold repair equipment for farming machines.

On one occasion and soon after the end of the first school semester, Superintendent Brian Scott received a call from Roger Moe. He indicated that he was at a local store pricing some equipment. Superintendent Scott replied, "You are doing what?"

Board Member Moe stated that he was "dealing" with the Fairview Equipment Company relative to discount prices on several pieces of equipment for use in the new vocational/tech program. He had worked with the company previously in his own personal business and was quite certain that he could get the best prices.

Superintendent Scott pointed out that the school district had a business office and a purchasing agent who took care of such matters. In addition, he explained that the state department had certain procedures for purchases related to vocational/technical programs and that equipment of a certain cost required a bidding process.

"Well," replied Mr. Moe, "You act as though you do not want me here. I'm just trying to do my job."

SNAPSHOT DISCUSSION

Although the school district and names of the individuals in the snapshot are fictitious, the situation in the case is true. What does the situation have to do with policy and regulations? What was missing in Moe's orientation for school board membership? What does the case infer regarding the up-front knowledge that a new school board member should possess? What does Moe need to learn about a school board member's authority when acting as an individual? Whose responsibility is it to inform a new member of school board procedures? How are the school board policies related to the case at hand? Consider the behavior of Superintendent Scott. Was Scott "professional" in his handling of this matter in your opinion? Why or why not?

The answers to the foregoing questions most often are revealed in one of the sections of an Alpha or Arabic codification system. For example, in section B of most Alpha systems, the topics of board member authority, board-staff communication, duties of members, board member development opportunities, and new member orientation are set forth.

As pointed out by Blumsack and McCabe (2016) in their discussion of effective school board members, as an individual, a school board member has no power to fix problems or to decide issues. The school board acts as a legislative body, not as an administrative one. Board members must refrain from trying to perform management functions that are the responsibility of the superintendent and staff.

The Saskatchewan School Boards Association (2016) notes that traditional school boards have governed with a high degree of hands-on involvement in the day-to-day management of local school systems. Today, many school boards are moving from a managerial emphasis to a policy development or strategic governance focus. In so doing, the school board:

- develops and articulates vision and goals;
- aligns resources to attain the goals;

- adopts policies to support achievement of the goals;
- establishes an accountability framework that measures progress toward goal achievement; and
- builds an effective leadership team.

Ballantyne & Associates (2006) called upon the collective wisdom and experience of many school board members to tell them what advice they found helpful when they joined their school boards. Ten selected responses were:

1. Get to know your role as a member of the school board, develop yourself in many ways, set goals for yourself, be positive, know your limits, and above all listen.
2. Do not be in a hurry to do something. It takes time to develop governance skills.
3. I am only one member of five voting members and not a power of one.
4. If you feel like you are overwhelmed, you are micromanaging.
5. Recognize the difference between policy and procedure.
6. Go to state association certified training as soon as possible.
7. I didn't realize that so much was prescribed in law.
8. I wish I would have known how best to communicate as a board member with the superintendent.
9. As a board member, you personally will not make any difference, but as a team, you will.
10. I wish I had known how easily misunderstood board decisions may be in the community and how important it is to overcommunicate.

Each of these responses has implications for the actions of the school board member in the foregoing snapshot. Arthur Griffin Jr. and Carter Ward (2006, March 21) wrote an article titled *Five Characteristics of an Effective School Board: A Multifaceted Role*. One of the five characteristics centered on policy development.

> The best school boards look for ways to institutionalize parent and patron involvement in providing policy-making input. Specifically, effective boards have established mechanisms for community involvement in setting the vision for the school district, representing the values of the community, and identifying the district's short-term and long-term priorities. (p. 1)

But School Board Members Do Not Get Paid, or Do They?

We found that the large majority of persons think that public school board members do not receive salaries, and they are right in the majority of cases. However, the situation among the states that do pay board members does vary. For example, reports indicate that the states of Florida, California, Virginia, North Carolina, and Alabama pay public school board members a salary. In New York, only the cities of Buffalo, New York City, Rochester, Syracuse, and Yonkers have salaries for school board members. In Florida, school board members receive $42,455 per year (White, not dated). In California, school board members earn $2,000 per month, but payment is based on student enrollment. New York State school board members reportedly receive varying salaries: one school district paid board members $5,000 annually; another, $23,000.

Some states pay school board members according to teachers' salaries, and monthly per diem payments are made for school board member activities in Michigan, Nevada, Ohio, Illinois, Missouri, New Jersey, and Louisiana. Per diem averages $100 to $200 per month. Salary payments are banned for board members in Texas, Pennsylvania, and Colorado. Although the large majority of school board members are voted into the position, in some cities such as New York City and Yonkers the school board members are appointed.

A FOCUS ON POLICY GOVERNANCE

Policy governance has been defined as an operating system that efficiently focuses boards on their unique contribution to the organization's results. Oliver (2016) notes that governance policies are organized under three headings: (1) Ends: The answers to the questions, what benefits is this organization to produce for which people and at what cost; (2) Executive Limitations: The answers to the limits of ethics and prudence to which the school executive must adhere; and (3) Governance Process: The board's definition of and rules for its own work. These factors promote purpose, integrity, and efficiency in governance and reflect as a distinct form of leadership.

The policy governance model differs from traditional policy governance. Its primary difference is vested in leadership. Traditional governance follows the procedure of approving actions presented by the school staff and then exercising its authority for managing the work of the school superintendent and staff. On the other hand, policy governance centers on the aims that the school system is to achieve. Follow-up activities center on evaluating and assessing the program results.

The Carver model centers on school board ownership, the board's responsibility for it, and its authority. As stated by authorities on the Carver model, governance policy is a shift from traditional governance in that it provides a clear differentiation between the governance and administrative responsibilities in organizations. The model is summarized by three primary school board responsibilities: (1) Ownership Linkage—connecting with and learning about the owners' values and the educational ends that are desired; (2) Policy Development—writing those values as policies as guidance for the organization and the school board itself; and (3) Assurance of Organizational Performance—monitoring to determine the progress being achieved toward the desired ends (Wikipedia, 2016, November 26).

The Carver Model of Policy Governance: In a Nutshell

In his detailed discussion of governance policy, Carver (2000) stated, "In light of leadership opportunities made possible by Policy Governance, governance as traditionally and widely practiced in all settings appears ill conceived, ineffective, and wasteful. . . . Our mission and our own integrity demand that boards govern rather than either rubber stamp or meddle. . . . Thus it is that most board training is merely teaching boards ho to do the wrong things better that they did them before" (pp. 2–3).

The five major purposes of a school board's job, according to Carver's governance policy model, are summarized in the following section. Note that a few entries have been changed to meet the conditions of education (e.g., CEO to superintendent, organization to school system, ownership to school community).

1. *The board's job.* It is the board's job to govern; the board has a commensurate to govern. Individual board members do not . . . whatever authority is legitimately wielded by a board is wielded by the board as a group . . . the school superintendent is bound by what the board says, but never by what any board member says. . . . That a board has its own job to do means, if the board is responsible for getting its own job done, that board agendas should be the board's agendas, not the superintendent's (CEO's) agenda.

2. *On behalf of the school community.* In any event, the board speaks in behalf of the owners (school community) and what their desires are, by (a) knowing the school community members and what their desires are, and (b) being able to distinguish and link with school community members.

3. *To see to it.* Means having a commitment that things come out right by (1) knowing the criteria that would signify success; (2) setting accountability for reaching the success criteria; and (3) systematically checking to see if the success criteria are being met; performance must be monitored regularly.

4. *Achieve what it should.* What should the school system achieve? What good is the school system to accomplish, for whom, at what cost or relative worth? Have the desired ends been achieved? Focus should be on the results to be achieved rather than the activities in which the school district has been engaged. Board members must learn that services, programs, and curricula have not value except that they produce the desired ends.

5. *Avoids what is unacceptable.* Carter recognizes the difficulty of stating that a school board should be focusing on ends rather than administrative management. Yet, he states that ultimately school boards are responsible for the means as well. He contends that school boards do have a way to deal with the dilemma by simply stating the means that are unacceptable. In fact, he states that the method works magically. The board states what is unacceptable and then gets out of the way. The contention is that the board avoids managing or meddling by not telling the school superintendent how to manage but telling him or her how not to manage. Carter's answer to this dilemma is by

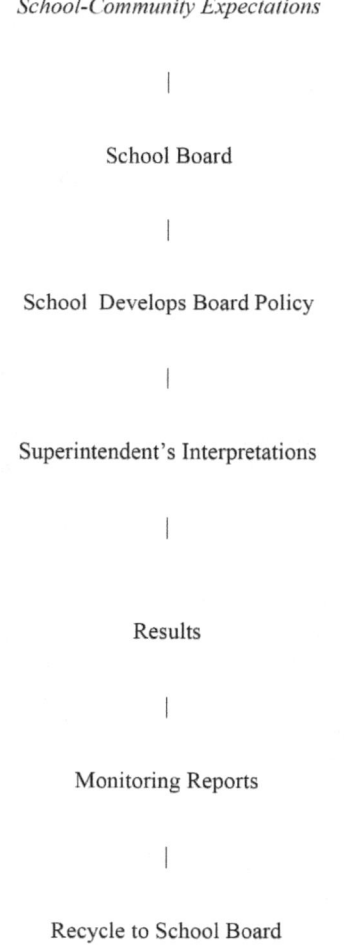

Figure 4.1

providing the leadership in (1) developing policies about ends; (2) developing policies that limit the superintendent's authority about methods, practices, situations, and conduct; (3) developing policies that prescribe how the board will govern itself; and (4) developing policies that delineate the manner in which governance is linked to management.

CRITICISM OF THE CARVER POLICY GOVERNANCE MODEL

As is common with most every innovative governance change, criticisms of the change come forth. In the case of the Carter governance policy model, arguments arise concerning leaving management matters solely to the administrators of the system. From a legal standpoint, state legislators have delegated certain legislative matters to the local school board. Both policy and regulations are included in such delegation. Therefore, to say that regulatory should not be part of management is questionable from a legal standpoint. In fact, school boards are obligated to be so involved. The arguments go on to say that school boards cannot escape direct responsibility to oversee the execution of policy.

Others argue that policy governance models are not applicable to all organizations; organizations differ widely. That is, the governance model tends to be ineffective in cases of crises when the executive branch of the system becomes troubled and/or ineffective. Because crises commonly occur within the administrative practices of the system, concentration on legislative matters is purposeless since the problems are rooted in current practice.

The statements that the school board is responsible for everything and then states that the model differentiates between ends and means is a puzzling contradiction. The model suggests that the school board should invest its efforts on the ends of the school district, not the means. Yet, the model's authorities have stated that the school board (organization) is responsible for the means as well. In related arguments, some suggest that the school board should not delegate any of its legal responsibility to the executive branch as previously noted. All too often, delegation of means by the school board occurs without adequate supervision.

WHAT ABOUT SCHOOL BOARD MEMBER QUALIFICATIONS?

In considering the responsibility for school board members to be the leaders of policy governance, the qualifications for doing so come into question.

Policy development, without question, is a challenging task. Even highly educated and experienced board members for leading organizations nationally contend that deciding on the purposes and ends of their work is among the most challenging features of their work. Would we expect a large business or industrial company to select board members who simply had expressed an interest in their product? Most likely we would select individuals who had a history of knowledge and experience in the organization's work.

The general role of school board members includes such responsibilities as determining school policies and direction, prioritizing the school district budget, giving final approval to hiring all personnel including the school superintendent, establishing an educational vision, making decisions about school expansion and/or closure, dealing with school bond issues, determining employee salaries, participating in collective bargaining, approving such daily operations as the school calendar, school contracts, adopting school curriculum, and other related duties.

Although the qualifications for school board membership do vary among the states, the most common requirements for membership include being able to read and write, being a citizen of the United States, being a resident of the school district for at least one year, being at least eighteen years of age, holding a high school diploma or certificate of equivalency, and *not* being judged as incompetent, convicted as a felon, residing with another member of the same school board, having been removed from any school district within the previous year, simultaneously holding another incompatible public office, or being a current employee of the district.

The point: Do the general requirements for school board membership have anything to do with the requirements of the job? Just how do the general requirements for school board membership square with the knowledge and skills required for developing a school district's governance policies and administrative regulations?

We asked one leading school superintendent his thoughts about school board member qualifications. He was fully aware that stating specific qualifications for school board membership is difficult, but he noted several questions that should be posed to those individuals who are interested in becoming a school board member. The superintendent's questions were as follows:

- What is your vision and what are your goals for high academic achievement for all students?
- Will you work to inspire parents and other stakeholders to have confidence in the local public schools?
- Do you understand that the school board's role is about the big picture—setting the direction for the school and providing oversight and accountability—rather than day-to-day management?

- Does your approach make it likely that you will be able to work effectively with the rest of the board to get things done?
- Will you enhance the mix of skills and backgrounds on the board and help represent diversity of the community?
- Do you have the commitment to do what's right for all children, even in the face of opposition?

We discuss school board qualifications again later in the chapter.

FURTHER THOUGHTS ABOUT CARVER'S GOVERNANCE MODEL

Carver's model that places policy development solely in the hands of a school board appears to be somewhat contrary to his perception of school boards generally. In his article on the school administrator (Carver, 2000, March), he stated: "Working with school boards can be harmful to one's health, as the longevity of superintendents may indicate, in part, because boards are the least disciplined, least rational and most disordered element in any school system. It seems obvious that administrators and teachers know their jobs immeasurably better than boards know theirs" (p. 1). So, let's place them totally in charge of school district policy, right?

In all fairness to Carver and his governance policy model, he notes that having dedicated, intelligent persons on boards does not correct the inadequacy. That is, his policy concepts and strategic policy model are the answer to the foregoing board problems. We tend to agree in part but believe that school board membership requirements are faulty at best; this topic will be discussed further in the recommendations section at the close of this chapter. At this point, we consider the characteristics of effective school boards.

AFFECTIVE AND COGNITIVE CHARACTERISTICS OF EFFECTIVE SCHOOL BOARDS

A review of the literature, interviews with various school personnel, and empirical evidence reveal several affective and cognitive characteristics of effective school boards:

- The school board places emphasis on effective policy development as it fosters, facilitates, and supports student learning. Policies set forth desired ends and give discretion that enable the school district leadership to implement their knowledge and skills for reaching the ends set forth.

- School district policy recommendations evolve from a variety of sources, and each is reviewed by the school board. Nevertheless, school policy governance most often is the result of the school board's efforts relative to achieving the values, desires of the school community, and the interests and needs of children and youth. In regard to effective school boards, school policy rather than administrative managements is the sine qua non of all actions of the school board.
- Ongoing monitoring of student achievement results is an important activity of the school board, but the collection of achievement progress is viewed as the responsibility of the school district professional staff. Policy support as opposed to achievement management is prevalent. Accountability in this regard is clearly stated in policy statements.
- Participative policy development is evidenced by effective school boards as opposed to public relations types of pronouncements and time-to-time input meetings. Making an effort to know the community is a priority that precedes school board policy decisions. Site-based councils consisting of parents, students, administrators, and representative community groups commonly are found in school districts with effective boards.
- Both basic and empirical research are important features of successful school boards. Program success, student achievement, public opinion, and assessment data are used to evaluate and assess program/policy results. Professional staff input alone is not viewed as sufficient by school boards that base policy decisions on data analysis.
- Effective/successful school boards have worked diligently to gain an understanding of school community cultures. In many instances, school boards have used survey strategies and study analyses, working alongside influential policy makers within the community, to determine school community values and beliefs. On the basis of such information and the values of school board members themselves, the school board's vision of educational purposes and ends is clearly established. In turn, a school superintendent is "researched" in terms of his or her qualities for working cooperatively with the board in achieving the desired ends.
- Personal/professional development is most often viewed as self-development on the part of members of successful school boards. Effective board members seek opportunities to become better contributors to the vision of the school board. Effective, relevant, and informative orientation programs are designed to support new board members but include ongoing development opportunities for all board members. Policy development along with board and administrative relations are found to be high priorities.

ELECTED VERSUS APPOINTED SCHOOL BOARDS: WHICH PROVIDES BETTER EDUCATION FOR STUDENTS?

Over the years, states have gone back and forth with arguments for or against elected and appointed school boards. The proponents of the elective process commonly contend that it is not only more democratic, but it also fosters more interest in the educational process and support of the community's schools. In addition, proponents point to the fact that elected boards are distanced from the politics that are apparent in appointed boards; education as opposed to municipal politics receives the major attention of board activities. In addition, elected board members are able to act more independently and can be held more accountable in the best interests of students.

Those favoring appointed boards argue that community members with the experience and skills required for successful school board operations can be sought for membership; most all appointees have the special skills needed for effective school board operations. In addition, persons in the community best qualified for board membership are reluctant to get involved in the problems related to election campaigns. Proponents of appointed school boards also argue that school elections usually attract very low voter turnout and therefore special-interest groups can easily be elected and dominate a school board. In addition, elections are costly. Who is to pay for them?

The debate on this matter has been brought to voters. Nevertheless, the implementation of appointed school boards or elected school boards continues to go back and forth. Historically, school boards have switched from an elected board to an appointed board and then back to an elected board. The movement, however, appears to be from appointed to elected boards.

Strangely enough, it seems as though a community with an elected school board often believes that an appointed board would be more productive and that the community with an elected board believes that an appointed board might serve them best. As reported by Van Tassel (1988), national studies indicated that no one system produces stronger school boards than the other.

CHAPTER SNAPSHOT

School Board Member and Staff Relationships

The Delta School District had just initiated a new educational program for physically handicapped students that included academic program instruction and physical therapy equipment. The new school assistant superintendent, Dr. Carson Monte, was put in charge of supervising all such programs in the school district and a department head, Dale Lemon, was hired to coordinate the physically handicapped program. He was to report to Dr. Monte.

Because the new educational program for the physically handicapped students was supported in part by the state department of education, certain procedural requirements for purchasing equipment were in place. For example, before any equipment costing more than $500 could be purchased, it had to be approved at the state level. If this procedure was not followed, the school district would not be refunded state monies of 50 percent of the purchase price. Dr. Monte had explained the purchasing requirements to Lemon both verbally and in writing.

Board member Len Sellers had special interest in the new program because his son, Homer, was physically handicapped and would be enrolled in the new program. Sellers had visited the program site on several occasions, and such visitations centered on the program provisions for his son.

After the third month of the new program's operations, Monte noted that equipment orders were being made without the required preapprovals. He immediately contacted Lemon and informed him that the purchasing procedures were in violation of state requirements, and refunds for such purchases could not be recouped. Lemon replied that the program needed the equipment, and the state's purchasing procedure was inhibiting program instruction.

Dr. Monte again explained that the school district did not have the budget to pay 100 percent of the equipment costs, and the loss of 50 percent of the equipment costs could not be tolerated. Purchasing procedures had to be followed thereafter.

During the next month, Monte visited the site of the new program and noticed a new piece of equipment with an approximate cost of $12,500 in one therapy room. Once again, Lemon had ordered the equipment without following the purchasing procedures. At an ensuing closed personnel meeting of the school board, Monte explained the purchasing problem with the board members, including his attempts to solve the problem with Lemon.

At that point, board member Sellers spoke out. He stated that he was informed of the need for equipment for the physically impaired on several occasions by Lemon. Lemon had made several visits to Seller's store and had told him of the ridiculous state purchasing requirement being enforced by Monte. Lemon said that Monte was just being stubborn and could move ahead on the purchases if he wanted to do so.

At that point in the meeting, board member Kenneth spoke up and said, "You mean that Lemon has been going directly to you for support on purchasing school equipment? Lemon was informed and then warned about the purchasing procedures, and he violated them anyway. A board member is only a citizen as an individual. Mr. Lemon has been insubordinate in surpassing his supervisor and purposely violating instructions." All other board members agreed.

SNAPSHOT DISCUSSION

What does the chapter snapshot tell us about school board member and staff relations? Lemon's behavior, without question, would be considered by the courts as insubordinate. Pryor (2015) points out that insubordination is the act of willfully disobeying an authority figure. "The typical way an employee gets into trouble for insubordination is by refusing to perform an action that their supervisor, or other authority figure requests" (p. 2). In the foregoing snapshot, Lemon was not only fully informed of the improper behavior, but outwardly refused to follow instructions.

One has to question the behavior of board member Sellers as well. Proper behavior would have been for him to ask Lemon at the outset if he had contacted the school superintendent relative to his concerns in this matter. We repeat the fact that meeting with a single board member carries no credibility for authoritative decisions.

On the other hand, Lemon would have been exercising his rights to question the purchasing procedure by indicating that he could not agree with it but would implement it as mandated. Protocol would recommend that Lemon inform Monte of his interest in discussing the matter with the school superintendent. Professional behavior in matters of procedural differences would be to obey an order of a supervisor until possible changes are made in the provision at hand.

CHAPTER 4 QUIZ

Chapter 4 closes with a statement of key ideas and recommendations, but first we present an opportunity for you to check your understanding of the concepts and information discussed in the chapter. For each question posed, give your best response, but do not guess the answer. Rather, go to the next question and then check your work with the discussion of the question answers that follow the quiz.

Chapter Quiz

1. A _____ is a rule recognized by the nation or state as being binding on its members.

    a. policy
    b. regulation
    c. bylaw
    d. law
    e. none of the above

2. Laws that emanate from governing bodies such as state legislatures are _____ _____ in a school board policy verbatim.

    a. never included
    b. commonly included
    c. always paraphrased
    d. alpha coded
    e. none of the above

3. Ultimately, the final decision for the legality of a school policy is determined by the _____ _____.

    a. school board
    b. state legislature
    c. school board association
    d. supreme court
    e. none of the above

4. The Fifth Amendment to the U.S. Constitution established the right of _____ _____.

    a. free speech
    b. due process
    c. bearing arms
    d. free education (to age eighteen)
    e. none of the above

5. The _____ _____ _____ in most states set forth advice on the policies and documents that governing bodies and proprietors of schools are required to have by law.

    a. state board of education
    b. school board association
    c. state legislature
    d. site-based council

6. One argument for local control of education is that it serves to improve the quality of _____ and _____ effectiveness.
7. A teacher's contract that specifies that the teacher will teach grade 1 is _____ _____ to teach grade 3 instead if asked to do so.
8. Policy governance models reportedly change the school board to one of _____ rather than one of _____.

a. followship rather than one of leadership
b. excellence rather than one of mediocrity
c. executive rather than one of legislative
d. leadership rather than one of followship
e. none of the above

9. Carter's Policy Development Model places emphasis on the school board being a _____ body.

   a. cooperative
   b. diverse
   c. management
   d. leadership
   e. none of the above

10. Effective school boards focus primarily on _____ and are responsible to the school district's _____.

    a. leadership/citizens
    b. administration/students
    c. management/patrons
    d. curriculum/students
    e. none of the above

11. Effective school boards are viewed as ones that focus on _____ to be achieved.

    a. standards
    b. ends
    c. regulations
    d. policies
    e. none of the above

12. The Carter Policy Model centers on _____ _____ _____.

    a. management strategies
    b. administrative regulations
    c. job performance
    d. policy codification
    e. none of the above

106   Chapter 4

13. _____ _____ has been defined as an operating system that efficiently focuses on their unique contributions to organizational _____.

   a. design
   b. practices
   c. management
   d. results

14. One criticism of the Carter Governance Model is that it contends that the school board does not focus on management but also states that it is responsible for all _____ as well.

   a. students
   b. ends
   c. means
   d. personnel
   e. none of the above

True or False

15. Empirical evidence suggests that local school districts pay approximately 74 percent of public school costs. ___T or ___F
16. Compliance centers on a school board's actions to obey the law. ___T or ___F
17. Empirical evidence suggests that 75 to 85 percent of public school districts develop and maintain their own educational policy systems. ___T or ___F
18. Although local control is an ongoing issue, no actions have been taken to return local control to school districts. ___T or ___F
19. Because school leaders are far more qualified to decide educational matters, chapter 4 recommends that school boards delegate policy development to the administrative staff of the school district. ___T or ___F
20. The courts have left all personnel matters related to insubordination to the local school superintendent. ___T or ___F

ANSWERS TO THE QUIZ

1. A *law* is a rule recognized by the nation or state as being binding on its members.
2. Laws that emanate from governing bodies, such as the state legislature, are *commonly included* in the school district's policy manual verbatim.

School districts tend to lose cases, such as student suspension and teacher dismissal, due to a failure to follow state statute mandates to the letter.
3. Ultimately, the final decision for the legality of a school board policy is determined by the *Supreme Court*. Such matters of student dress and the wearing of certain emblems/sayings on clothing have reached the U.S. Supreme Court.
4. The Fifth Amendment to the U.S. Constitution establishes the right of *due process*. This amendment also forbids "double jeopardy" and self-incrimination along with requiring due process in cases of denial of a citizen's life, liberty, or property.
5. The *Department of Education* in most states sets forth advice on the policies and documents that governing bodies and proprietors of schools are required to have by law.
6. One argument for local control is that it improves the quality of *teaching* and *learning* effectiveness. Other pros and cons relative to local control were set forth in chapter 4.
7. A new teacher contracted to teach grade 1 is *not required* to teach grade 3 if the need exists. Of course, the teacher can be assigned to other elementary school grades if he or she agrees to do so.
8. Policy Governance models change the school board from a position of *followship* to *leadership*. This change recommends that school boards begin to assume the leadership for policy development rather than merely reacting to policies set forth by the school superintendent or other individuals or groups.
9. The Policy Governance Model emphasizes the school board as a *leadership* body. As noted in the previous question, school boards are to assume the development of policies as opposed to reacting to policies submitted by others or purchasing boilerplate policies from external sources.
10. Effective school boards focus primarily on *leadership* and are responsible to the school district's *citizens*. As recommended by such governance policy as the Carter model, the owners of the organization serve as the primary resources for policy development.
11. Effective school districts are viewed as ones that focus on the *ends* to be achieved. Aims, goals, purposes, results, and ends serve as the primary focus for school board policy development.
12. The Carter Policy Model centers on *none of the above*. See #8, #9, and #11 above.
13. *Policy governance* has been defined as an operational system that efficiently focuses on the unique contribution of organizational *results*.
14. One criticism of Carter's Governance Model is that the school board does not focus on management but also states that it is responsible for all *means*. This aspect of the Carter model presents the need for additional

questioning. Examine the chapter reference of Carter and Oliver for additional clarification on this matter.
15. Empirical evidence suggests that school districts pay approximately 74 percent of educational cost is *False*. A more accurate figure would be 46 percent according to educational research statistics.
16. Compliance centers on school board's actions to obey the law is *True*.
17. Empirical evidence would not support the statement that 75 to 85 percent of school districts maintain their own policy governance system. In fact, total support of policy systems in school districts would be extremely low, especially if school districts that used the services of state/national school boards associations were excluded. We dare say that no more than 10 percent of school districts in the United States have school policy systems devoid of external support.
18. Although local control is an ongoing issue, no actions have been taken to return local control to school districts is *False*. A local policy bill was drafted in Congress recently, and some states such as New Jersey have been granted partial local control of some aspects of school policy (e.g., personnel).
19. Because school leaders are far more qualified to decide educational matters, chapter 4 recommends that school boards delegate policy development to the administrative staff of the school district is *False*. No such action to our knowledge ever has been considered.
20. The courts have left all personnel matters related to insubordination to the local school superintendent is *False*. On the contrary, insubordination cases have been decided in many court cases nationally.

KEY CHAPTER IDEAS AND RECOMMENDATIONS

- There are two sides of the legal equation in regard to public school education—compliance and maintenance of updated and accurate governance policies to avoid legal problems, plus taking the leadership for developing policy that establishes the educational ends to be achieved in relation to student learning.
- Local control of education means the state is responsible for establishing the purposes/aims of education, leaving discretion for the local school district to determine the administrative provisions for achieving the desired ends.
- There are pros and cons related to the concept of local control of education. State legislatures and local school districts should focus on the strengths of local control provisions and work with each other to balance the cons related to the concept.

- The primary recommendation today is for school boards to practice leadership as opposed to followship in the development and implementation of school district policies.
- Effective school boards can indeed be identified. Attention to the school board's responsibility for policy development is at the top of the list of positive characteristics.
- The need for a serious examination and review of the qualifications for school board membership is long overdue. No organization can be successful without having highly knowledgeable and skilled board members. Present "qualifications" for school board membership do not meet the knowledge and skill requirements for the role. We believe that a full examination of the basic knowledge and skill requirements be taken and appropriate requirements for qualified board membership be implemented.

Rather than national and state school board associations drafting boilerplate policies that commonly are duplicated in all districts, state school board associations, school administrator associations, and other educational groups should focus on the matter of school board membership and the basic qualities that are needed/advisable for participating on a school board. Such a statement of qualifications could be tied to a required licensure program before an individual is able to assume a position on a school board; after-the-fact development and attempts to learn on the job do not provide the foundation for effective performance of the work required in one of the most important priorities for America's future: education of students.

It is true that state school board associations provide many growth programs for school board members, but such provisions tend to be after the fact. We propose a before-the-fact procedure whereby a certification or licensure requirement be required for potential school board members. That is, such development programs should be front-loaded as pre-training as opposed to after-the-fact post-training. One might argue that it can't be done. It's done with most every professional position in education today, and school board membership should be no exception.

Thought has to be given to how such a certification program is administered and by whom. Several existing agencies, with certain changes such as programs within universities and colleges, county superintendent offices, or state school board associations, might gear up to do the task. Consideration must be given to continuing the development program after the individual has been elected to a board position. Most states require certain staff development for teachers and administrators; similar development should be required for school board members. The curriculum for such programs would focus on what factors are demonstrated by effective school boards and school board members such as those set forth in chapter 3.

Impossible? We do not believe so. Revolutionary, perhaps, but essential. We contend that unless such a "before-the-fact" program for school board members is required, the trail to board governance leadership will continue to be one of followship.

DISCUSSION QUESTIONS

1. Give some consideration to the last entry in the section on Key Chapter Ideas and Recommendations. Then assume that you are a school superintendent and a representative on the advisory committee of the state's school board association. The committee has been discussing the matter of school board effectiveness. Set forth your input relative to the question at hand: "What qualifications should be required for school board membership?"
2. Take a stand on the matter of school boards purchasing their school policies from the state school board association. As a professional school administrator, take a position for or against on the matter. Be as specific as possible in your response. "I don't care" is an unacceptable answer.
3. Assume that you personally are a new school board member. You begin your service in two months. What information do you need and want to know? What sources might you pursue to find the information that you desire?
4. Consider the policy concepts of the Carter Governance Model. What two or three concepts do you recall that differentiate the GP model from the traditional governance model?
5. Local control of education has been a specific topic for this book and is discussed in depth in chapter 4. State and federal mandates have been the center of the "arguments" for returning education to the control of local school districts. One contention is that local control will result in improved teaching and learning in school settings. Take a pro or con position on the foregoing "argument." Give reasons/evidence for your stand.
6. Give thought to the work of the school board. In your opinion, should school board members receive a commensurate annual salary—yes or no? Support your answer with some rationale. For example, would a commensurate salary serve to encourage more highly qualified persons to seek the position?

CASE STUDY

Let's Just Wait and See

Elaine Morton, a school board member of the Viewpark School District, has just returned from attending a conference sponsored by the state board of education on policy and regulation development. The focus of the conference centered on an "expected" legislative mandate that would require all school districts to have evidence of an effective school policy system in place within the next two years. Although the school board had a policy manual in place, it consists mainly of boilerplate policies that were purchased by the district from the local school board association.

Elaine Morton was of the opinion that the governance system discussed at the conference had positive implications for improving the Viewpark policy system and asked Orin Doolittle, the school board chair, if a study session might be organized for the purposing of considering policy development improvements. She felt that she had captured the perspective of the state board on the matter and could bring it to any follow-up activity. One thing appeared to be certain: the state department of education did not favor purchasing school board policies as an improvement strategy.

Kathryn Scott, superintendent, received a call from Orin Doolittle, who informed her of the policy matter. He asked Scott her opinion about the situation because he valued her opinion. Scott was rather cold to the idea and stated that the state board seemed to have its hand in local school matters more and more over the past few years. They usually just fade away.

"The state board did the same thing with special education, the gifted program and achievement standards, but after all of our time and effort, these things seem to fall through the cracks and we are left with requirements with no financial support to sustain them. I just wish that they would leave us alone; after all, we are the professionals," stated Superintendent Scott.

As expected, the state board of education adopted a regulation that required all school districts to have an effective policy system in place and to submit their plans to the department of education for approval.

When board chairman Doolittle received the state board's notification, he asked two other school board members and Superintendent Scott to write up the policy improvement plan. Elaine Morton was not asked to be involved.

Discussion Questions

1. Did chairman Doolittle make a good decision? Why or why not?
2. What problems might be anticipated from the board chairman's decision?
3. Does Elaine Morton have any options she might take? For example, might she submit her notes on the policy conference to the board chairman? What are your recommendations as to what board chair Doolittle should do?
4. What might be the consequences from Doolittle's decision to ask Superintendent Scott to serve on the committee?
5. Is this case study typical in any way? What is your opinion?

REFERENCES

Arkansas School Boards Association (2006, April 5). *Developing and adopting school board policy*, chap. 4. Little Rock, AR: Author.

Ballantyne, J. (2006). *The primary difference between traditional governance and policy governance*, governing.ca/traditional.html.

Bell, T. (1988). Parting of the 13th man. *Phi Delta Kappan* 69, 400–407.

Blumsack, K., & McCabe, T. (2016, July/August). 7 practices of highly effective board members. *American School Board Journal.*

Carver, J. (2000). Toward coherent governance. *The school administrator.* American Association of School Administrators, Alexandria, VA.

Center for Public Education (2006, April 5). *The laws and its influence of public school districts: An Overview.* Alexandria, VA: National School Boards Association.

Griffin, A. Jr., & Ward, C. (2006, March 26). "Five characteristics of an effective school board: A multifaceted role." Edutopia, George Lucas (ed.). Nicasio, CA.

New Jersey State Board of Education (2016). *New Jersey State Board of Education approves resolution to return functions of fiscal management & personnel to local control in the Patterson Public School District*, Patterson.K12.nj.us/news/15–16–/02–11–OSAC%202016%20Release%20Final.pdf.

Norton, M. S. (2008). *Human resources administration for educational leaders.* Thousand Oaks, CA: Sage.

Oliver, C. (2016, November, 26). *Policy governance differs from traditional governance.* Shaking Foundation of Governance. A discussion forum hosted by the UK Policy Governance Association and the CRSA Forum.

Peterson, L. J., Rossmiller, R. A., & Volz, M. M. (1978). *The law and public school operation.* New York: Harper & Row.

Pryor, B. D. (2015, June 30). *Insubordination: When do you have to do what you're told . . . And when don't you?* Chicago: Cook County College Teachers Union, Local 1600.

Saskatchewan School Boards Association (2016). *A pathway to effective board policy governance, module 5.* Regina, Saskatchewan, saskschoolboards.ca/wp-content/uploads/2015/08/Module_5__Effective__Board__Policy__Governance.pdf.

State Board of Education (2016, August 3). *State board of education returns an additional category of local control to Newark, moving the district closer to full local control.* Trenton, NJ.

Van Tassel, P. (1988, November 6). *School boards: Elected or appointed? New York Times,* nytimes.com/1988/11/06/nyregion/school-boards-elected-or-appointed.html?pagewanted=2.

White, R. (not dated). *What states have salaried school board members?* ehow contributor, www.ehow.com/info_states-salaried-school-board-members.html.

Wikipedia (2016). *Policy governance*, en.Wikipedia.org/wiki/Policy-Governance.

Glossary

Academic Freedom: Includes the right of teachers to speak freely about their subject, to experiment with new ideas, and to select appropriate teaching materials and methods without unreasonable interference or restriction from law, institutional regulations, or public pressure.

Administrative Regulation: A precise statement that answers the question of how a policy is to be applied or implemented.

Alpha Codification System: The school board policy classification system developed by the National Association of School Boards using the alphabet for coding entries. The coding system commonly includes a series of eight to nine sections with subsections, divisions, subdivision, items, and sub-items.

Analysis Approach: An approach used to identify a school community's power structure by determining the persons who are most often identified in decisions relative to important issues in the school community.

Arabic Codification System: The school board policy classification system developed by Davies and Brickell using Arabic numbers for coding entries.

Bylaws: Procedures by which the school board governs itself.

Carter Governance Policy Model: A model for governance that places the local school board in the position of leadership rather than followup relative to school policy development.

Certificated Personnel: Employees such as teachers and administrators who are officially licensed and accredited for the positions they hold.

Classified Personnel: Noncertificated personnel who serve the school district.

Codification System: The coding of policies and regulations for purposes of classification.

Common Core: The federal mandates set forth for curriculum provisions, achievement standards, and instructional methods for programs in public schools that are receiving federal funding.

Compliance: Conformity in fulfilling official requirements. Refers to the duty of school boards to obey the law and take steps to be in compliance with it.

Conflict of Interest: A conflict of interest is present or occurs when a school board member or member of the school staff is in a position of deciding on a policy and/or influencing the result of a contract award that holds benefits for the member.

Corporation: An incorporated political subdivision of a state that is composed of citizens of a designated geographic and that performs certain state functions on a local level and possesses such powers as are conferred upon it by the state.

Court: Government entity authorized to resolve legal disputes.

Cultural Sanctions: The traditional beliefs, values, traditions, and requirements that a group of people or community holds as essential to the goals of their behaviors and governance decisions.

Davies-Brickell Codification System: The foundational system of classifying policies using numbers for coding purposes. The system commonly has a series of nine sections from 1000 to 9000 accompanied by subsections, divisions, subdivisions, items, and sub-items.

Due Process: The provision of protecting an individual's rights relative to alleged violations by using such features as notice, the right of a hearing, the right to be represented by counsel, and other legal protections.

Elite Power Structure: The case whereby an elite group of individuals within the community tend to control school board decisions. In some cases, the power structure consists of only 2 to 5 percent of the community members. In some cases, the true "generals" of the power structure are always behind the scenes and work their influence through the lieutenants who are more prevalent in the community.

External Control: The impact of federal laws, state statutes, and court rulings that tend to control matters of school programming, teaching procedures, and student provisions that tend to inhibit the ability of the district school board to make local decisions on such matters.

External Influences: The various influences on such matters as school policy development and program decision by outside agencies such as federal laws, state statutes, court rulings, and power groups.

Factional Power Structure: The case whereby the power of the school board is spread among factions that vie for control of decisions about important issues facing the school community.

Followship: A term introduced by Ballantyne (2006) in relation to his discussions on policy governance. The term, not in the dictionary, is used as being opposed to the term leadership (note: followership might have been a more appropriate term).

Governance Policy Model: The Carver Governance Model serves to establish the school board as the leader in the development of school policies for governing the school district. That is, the school board is to take the leadership for developing the policies rather than receiving recommended policies drafted by the school superintendent/staff and then acting on them.

Governing Board Policy: Governing school board policies are comprehensive statements of decisions, principles, or courses of action to be applied or implemented. A policy serves to answer the question of what to do; it focuses on the ends to be achieved and leaves discretion for the professional staff to determine how the policy is to be implemented.

Hearing: A process for providing due process to a student, teacher, or classified employee in relation to a violation of school board policies and/or administrative regulations. The due process in such instances commonly is established by state statutes and included verbatim in the school board's policy manual.

Inert Power Structure: A form of school board power that is latent or inactive. The school board depends on the school superintendent for policy development and serves to approve what the school superintendent recommends.

Law: A rule recognized by the nation or state as binding on its members.

Local Control: The ability of local school boards and their personnel to have the authority to make important decisions relative to school policies, administrative regulations, instructional methods, and curricular programming.

Maintenance: The upkeep of a system or property such as a policy system.

National School Board Association's Codification System: The policy classification system developed by NSBA in 1971 and used by the large majority of school districts in the United States for classification purposes of their policy systems.

NJQSAC: The New Jersey Quality Single Accountability Continuum. The state's school monitoring system that serves as a framework to evaluate districts in five separate functional areas: Governance, Fiscal Management, Personnel, Operations, and Instruction.

On-Base System: A system for storing school records.

Phased Retirement: Any human resources program that allows older/experienced workers to reduce their work hours without changing employers and eases the transition into retirement.

Pluralistic Power Structure: The school community power structure that exists within the school board that features a variety of reasonable and dedicated individuals who act in a cooperative and democratic manner in studying and acting on school matters.

Policy Adoption: The official process used by the school board to approve a policy as a legal action. Only the school board can approve school policies.

Policy Series: The major heading/topics included in a school board's policy system. These policy manual headings do differ to some extent among school districts but commonly include such headings such as school district operations, administration, personnel, business, students, instruction, community relations, and construction/facilities.

Policy System: The action taken by a school board to design and maintain an effective strategy for implementing an ongoing effective program for policy and regulation development.

Power Structure: A group or single individuals in the school community who use their position and/or power to influence policy decisions relative to what will or what will not be decided or adopted by the school board.

Prevention: The actions taken by the school board to avoid legal problems, including compliance with it.

Procedure: The rules for conducting a lawsuit; there are rules of civil procedure, bankruptcy, and appellate procedure.

Quasi-Corporation: Generally, an entity that exercises some of the functions of a corporation but has not been granted separate legislative personality by statute. A school board is considered a quasi-corporation.

Reputational Approach: The strategy used to identify the power structure within the school community using the "reputation" of influential individuals.

Rule: Is most commonly viewed as a requirement set forth by a local school that centers on student behavior, attendance requirements, student dress, and other behaviors required of students. School rules are often incorrectly referred to as "our school policies." Rules commonly extend from the school district's administrative regulations.

School Board Policy: Comprehensive statements of decisions, principles, or courses of action that serve toward the achievement of stated educational goals. Policies answer the question of what it is the school program is to accomplish.

Sine qua non: An absolutely indispensable or essential thing; without which not.

Statute: Law enacted by the legislative power of a county or state.

Student Expulsion: The act of depriving a student of the right of membership in the school for some violation or offense that renders him or her unworthy of remaining a member of the school.

Student Suspension: The exclusion of a student from school for a brief but definite period of time.

REFERENCES

Ballantyne, J. (2005). *The primary difference between traditional governance and policy governance*, governing.ca/traditional.html.

About the Author

Dr. M. Scott Norton is a former public school mathematics teacher, coordinator of curriculum, assistant superintendent, and superintendent of schools. He served as professor and vice chair of the Department of Educational Administration and Supervision at the University of Nebraska, Lincoln, later becoming professor and chair of the Department of Educational Administration and Policy Studies at Arizona State University, where he is currently professor emeritus. His primary graduate research and instruction areas include classes in human resources administration, the school superintendency, the school principalship, educational leadership, curriculum/instruction, the assistant school principal, research methods, organizational development, and competency-based administration.

Dr. Norton is the author and/or coauthor of college textbooks in the areas of school superintendency, competency-based leadership, the principal as a student advocate, the school principal as a learning leader, great teachers, the legal world of the school principal, the assistant school principal, curriculum and supervision, and administrative management. He has published widely in national journals in such areas as teacher retention, teacher load, retention of quality school principals, organizational climate, classified personnel in schools, employee assistance programs, distance education, gifted student programs, student retention, and others.

Four other books written by Dr. Norton and published by Rowman & Littlefield include *The Principal as a Learning Leader: Motivating Students by Emphasizing Achievement*, *Competency-Based Leadership: A Guide for High Performance in the Role of the School Principal*, *Teachers with the Magic: Great Teachers Change Students' Lives*, and *The Legal World of the School Principal*. One of his coauthored books, *Resources Allocation: Managing Money and People*, was published by Eye on Education. Two other books, *The School Principal as a Human Resources Leader* and *The Assistant Principal's Guide: New Strategies for New Responsibilities*, were published by Routledge in 2015. His most recent book is *Guiding Curriculum Development: The Need to Return to Local Control*, and *Guiding the School District's Human Resources Function* has just gone to press.

He has received several state and national awards honoring his services and contributions to the field of educational administration from such organizations as the American Association of School Administrators, University Council for Educational Administration, Arizona Administrators Association, Arizona Educational Research Association, Arizona State University College of Education Dean's Award for excellence in service to the field, president of the ASU College of Education Faculty Association, and the distinguished service award from the Arizona Information Service.

Dr. Norton's state and national leadership positions have included service as executive director of the Nebraska Association of School Administrators, member of the board of directors for the Nebraska Congress of Parents and Teachers, president of the Nebraska Council of Teachers of Mathematics, president of the Arizona School Administrators Higher Education Division, member of the Arizona School Administrators Board of Directors, staff associate of the University Council for School Administrators, treasurer of the University Council for School Administrators, Nebraska state representative for the National Association of Secondary School Principals, and member of the board of editors for the American Association of School Public Relations.

www.ingramcontent.com/pod-product-compliance
Lightning Source LLC
Chambersburg PA
CBHW021852300426

44115CB00005B/135